Healthcare Defensive Tactics System™
Student Manual

David Fowler

Founder and Author of
Healthcare Defensive Tactics System™ Training Programs

healthcare defensive tactics system

Student Manual

Healthcare Defensive Tactics System™ Training

ISBN: 978-1534920958

Printed in the United States of America

Personal Safety Training Inc.
P.O. Box 2957
Coeur d' Alene, ID 83816 USA
Telephone: (208) 664-5551
www.PersonalSafetyTraining.com

Also by David Fowler

Defense Baton™ Training Program
Defensive Tactics System™ Training Program
Healthcare Defensive Tactics System™
Handcuffing Tactics™ Training Program
Security Incident Reporting System™
Security Oriented Customer Service Training Manual
AVADE® Instructor Manual
AVADE® Advanced Student Guide
AVADE® Basic Student Guide
Violence In The Workplace
Violence In The Workplace II
Be Safe Not Sorry
To Serve and Protect

Acknowledgement

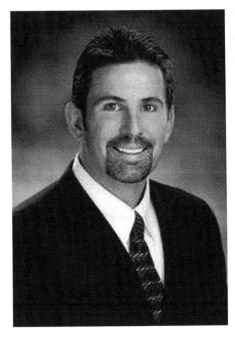

I would like to thank the many teachers, instructors, mentors and friends that have helped make this program a reality. Without your help, inspiration and invaluable knowledge this wouldn't have been possible. To all of you, I am eternally grateful.

I would also like to thank the thousands of individuals that I have worked with whose direct and indirect contribution to this program has made it possible for me to do what I feel on purpose to do.

Special thanks to the following individuals for their support and technical advice: Jason Blessinger, Jean Boles, Mark Costello, Genelle Fowler, Brian Goodwin, Brian Keltz, Mark Loudin, Steve Petillo, Eduardo Montez and Mark Mooring.

I would also like to thank my family for their support; I love you all so much!

David

David Fowler
Founder, Healthcare Defensive Tactics System Training
President, Personal Safety Training Inc.

Healthcare Defensive Tactics System™ Training Program
Student Registration Form (Please Print Clearly)

Course Title: **8 hour** ☐   **Modular** ☐

Course Trainer: _____

Date(s): _____

Safety and Waiver Agreement

Student Name: _____

Agency/Title: _____

Address: _____

City/State/Zip: _____

Telephone: _____

Work E-mail: _____

In signing this agreement it serves as a release from liability and assumption of risk.

1. I am in good physical and mental health.

2. I have no reason to believe that I am not in good physical and mental health.

3. I am fully aware of and do acknowledge and assume all risk of injury inherent in my participation in the HDTS™ - Healthcare Defensive Tactics System™.

4. I have read and fully understand the terms and conditions of this agreement.

5. I hereby waive and release Personal Safety Training Inc. (HDTS™ - Healthcare Defensive Tactics System™) for any physical and/or mental injury suffered by me during any and all training activities in the HDTS™ - Healthcare Defensive Tactics System™.

Signature: _____ **Date(s):** _____

Trainers Use Only

Written Test Score: _____   **Skills Test:** _____

Re-Test Score: _____   **Skills Test Retest:** _____

Trainers Signature of completion: _____

Although every effort has been made for the training course, manuals, and related materials to be complete and accurate, it is impossible to predict, discuss or plan for every circumstance or situation which might arise in the course of training and in any contact with a violent or aggressive person(s) or for a crime. Every trainee must always take into consideration their experience, physical abilities, professional responsibilities, agency and department procedures and state, local and federal legal requirements. With this in mind, each trainee must evaluate the recommendations and techniques contained in the training course, manuals, and related material, and decide for himself (herself) which should be used and under what circumstances. Each trainee assumes risk of loss, injury, and damages associated with this training and use of the information obtained through the Healthcare Defensive Tactics System™ training course or any Personal Safety Training Inc. training courses. **Personal Safety Training Incorporated cannot guarantee or warrant the training, the manuals or any related materials. Any implied warranties are expressly disavowed**.

Contents

Introduction

Introduction to the Healthcare Defensive Tactics System™ (HDTS™)

In today's society, law enforcement, security, corrections, military and protective services agencies realize that defensive tactics strategies and techniques are essential for protecting themselves and the public that they serve. These agencies also understand that mitigating liability begins with proper training and education in defensive tactics strategies and techniques.

The Healthcare Defensive Tactics System™ is a training program designed for public safety officers to reduce the potential of injury and liability risk when lawfully defending themselves or controlling an aggressive individual. The tactics and techniques in this training curriculum are for incidents where the aggressor is physically resistive and unarmed.

This training manual, for the Healthcare Defensive Tactics System™, provides training and education that is designed to empower officers, increase awareness, knowledge, skills and actions with regard to use of force, control and restraint, self-defense, and defending others with defensive tactics strategies and techniques.

This course stresses the importance of knowing your agency policies and procedures in regard to using force and defending yourself or another person. The Healthcare Defensive Tactics System™ training is intended to give the trainee the basic understanding of self-defense, use of force, control and restraint, reasonable force and basic legal definitions of force. Personal Safety Training Inc. makes no legal declaration, representation or claim as to what force should be used or not used during a self-defense, use of force incident or assault incident or situation. Each trainee must take into consideration their ability, agency policies and procedures and laws in the state and country in which they reside

The techniques in this training course are uncomplicated for most individuals to learn and develop proficiency. Basic defensive tactics fundamentals are taught followed by contact and cover positioning, escort strategies & techniques, control & decentralization, handcuffing techniques, defensive blocking techniques, personal defense skills & techniques, weapon retention techniques and post incident response and documentation procedures.

This course is modular based and can be taught over a period of one year or less to achieve a certificate of competency. Or, it can be taught in its entirety, in an eight hour basic course to achieve a certificate of competency.

> ### Special Note:
> **Defensive tactics are considered use of force options for unarmed attacks and are not intended to replace firearms, chemical sprays, electronic stunning devices, or any authorized piece of equipment that officers use to defend against situations involving weapons or multiple attackers.**

First Rule of Training = Safety

Before taking part in any physical training YOU must understand the safety rules.

- **Weapons Free environment:** No weapons are allowed anywhere in the training area. Instructor will advise participants in proper procedures in securing weapons and ammunition. Follow agency policy and procedures.

- **Remove jewelry, etc.:** The following should not be worn during a class which involves hands-on training: all jewelry with sharp edges; pins or raised surfaces; or jewelry that encircles the neck.

- **No Horseplay Rule:** Any participant who displays a disregard for SAFETY to anyone in class will be asked to leave the class. Please practice only the technique currently being taught. **DO NOT PRACTICE UNAUTHORIZED TECHNIQUES**

- **Pat out Rule (used for control techniques):** Upon hearing/feeling/seeing the "PAT," your partner applying the technique will immediately release the pressure of the technique to reduce discomfort/pain. The technique will be immediately and totally released on instructions from the instructor or when a safety monitor says "RELEASE," "STOP," or words similar to them.

- **Be a Good, "Good Guy" and a "Good Bad Guy":** Essentially this means working together with your partner when practicing the techniques. Without cooperation while practicing self-defense or defensive control tactics techniques, time is wasted and injury potential is increased. Work together to learn together!

- **Check equipment for added safety:** The instructor will check all equipment used during the training to ensure proper function, working order and safety.

- **Practice techniques slowly at first:** Gain balance and correctness slowly before practicing for speed. Proceed at the pace directed by your trainer.

- **Advise instructor of ANY pre-existing injuries:** Any injury or condition that could be further injured or aggravated should be brought to the immediate attention of your instructor, and your partner, prior to participating in any hands-on training.

- **Advise instructor of ANY injury during class:** Any injury, regardless of what it is, needs to be reported to the primary instructor.

- **Safety is EVERYONE'S responsibility!:** Safety is everyone's responsibility and everyone is empowered to immediately report or YELL OUT any safety violation or concern about safety.

- **Training Hazards:** Always keep any items or training equipment and batons off the floor/ground and out of the way when not in use. They are potential tripping/fall hazards.

- **Safety Markings:** USE CAUTION WITH A PARTNER WHO IS WEARING A COLORED WRIST BAND OR RED/BLUE TAPE.

- **STRETCHING:** A low-impact stretching, from head to toe can prevent possible injuries and strains. Keep eyes open, avoid jerking and bouncing, and breathe.

Modular Based Training

The Healthcare Defensive Tactics System™ Training is a modular based training program which can be taught in an eight-hour basic course or presented modularly during roll call, safety or departmental meetings throughout a 12-month period.

Healthcare Defensive Tactics System™

- **Use of Force**
- **Defensive Tactics Fundamentals**
- **Contact and Cover Positioning**
- **Escort Strategies & Techniques**
- **Control & Decentralization Techniques**

Healthcare Defensive Tactics System™

- **Handcuffing Techniques**
- **Defensive Blocking Techniques**
- **Personal Defense Skills & Techniques**
- **Weapon Retention Techniques**
- **Post Incident Response/Documentation**
- **Healthcare Restraint Holds/Application**

Modules and Objectives

1. **Use of Force and Self-Defense:** Mitigate liability risk through proper documentation and the understanding of use of force and defense of one's self or others.

2. **Defensive Tactics Fundamentals:** Provide proper knowledge and education of defensive tactics fundamentals and techniques.

3. **Contact and Cover Positioning:** Increase awareness and understanding of initial contact, proper positioning, and using contact and cover strategies.

4. **Escort Strategies and Techniques:** Provide knowledge and awareness of how to effectively and safely escort an individual with one or more persons.

5. **Control & Decentralization Techniques:** Reduce the potential for injury and assault through proper understanding of control and decentralization techniques for dealing with physically aggressive individuals.

6. **Handcuffing Techniques:** Teach effective methods for handcuffing individuals in a standing, kneeling or prone position.

7. **Defensive Blocking Techniques:** Provide defensive blocking techniques from attacks to various areas of the body.

8. **Personal Defense Skills & Techniques:** Provide defensive intervention skills and techniques to counter attacks and bring an aggressive individual under control.

9. **Personal Weapon Retention Techniques:** Teach safety tips and techniques for effectively retaining your personal weapon from being taken or used against you.

10. **Post Incident Documentation:** Provide methods, techniques and systems for post incident response and documentation.

11. **Healthcare Restraint Holds/Applications:** Mitigate liability risk through proper understanding of restraint holding techniques and application of restraints.

Module One – Use of Force and Self-Defense

Any use of force or self-defense intervention must be reasonable and legally justified.

Awareness of "LIABILITY RISK"

When any force is used, the officer MUST take into consideration their ability, agency policies and procedures and laws in the state and country in which they reside.

Unauthorized or inappropriate use of force or defense may expose the officer and/or agency to criminal and/or civil liability.

Personal Safety Training Inc. does not dictate policies or procedures for arrest, detention, control and restraint, self-defense, use of force or any physical intervention authorized for use by a department/agency or private individual. The suggestions, options and techniques disseminated during this training program are simply that, suggestions, options and techniques. Each individual, department or agency is responsible for developing their own "policies and procedures" regarding use of force, self-defense, physical intervention, physical restraints, physical control, arrest and detention for their personnel.

Agency Policies and Procedures

What are YOUR policies and procedures for use of force and self-defense?

_____

_____

_____

_____

_____

_____

Officers should have a strong understanding of their agency policies and procedures regarding use of force and self-defense.

_____

_____

_____

_____

_____

_____

What is Self-Defense?

Self-defense is the right to use reasonable force to protect one's self or members of one's staff/family from bodily harm from the attack of an aggressor, if you have reason to believe that you or they are in danger.

ATTITUDE

"Self Defense"
Do you have the right?
How does it apply?
1. Avoid
2. Get Away
3. Defend

Last Resort
Reasonable

Individuals do have the right to self-defense. The application must follow any agency policy and procedure as well as state and federal law. The best self-defense is to avoid the situation and get away. If avoidance and escape are not possible a reasonable defense would be lawful as a last resort.

The following information will provide a general understanding of self-defense and use-of-force, so that you can legally protect yourself against liability risks associated with any type of self-defense and/or use of force.

Use-of-Force

Use-of-Force: A term that describes the right of an individual or authority to settle conflicts or prevent certain actions by applying measures to either:

- **Dissuade another party from a particular course of action…or**
- **Physically intervene to stop or control them.**

Disclaimer: This module is intended to give the trainee the basic understanding of self-defense, use of force, reasonable force and basic legal definitions of force. Personal Safety Training Inc. makes no legal declaration, representation or claim as to what force should be used or not used during a self-defense, use of force incident, or assault incident or situation. Each trainee must take into consideration their ability, agency policies and procedures and laws in the state and country in which they reside.

Lawful Use of Force and Self-Defense

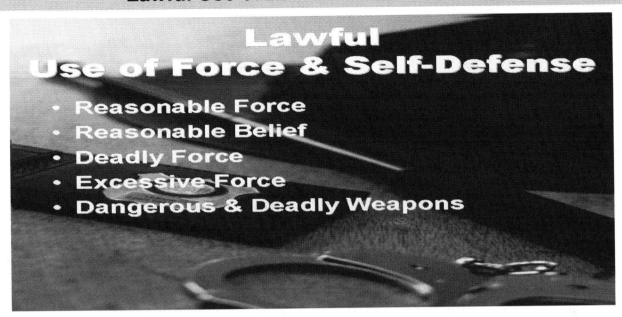

Reasonable Force
✓ The degree of force which is not excessive and is appropriate in protecting oneself, members of one's family/staff or one's property.

✓ When such force is used, a person is justified and is not criminally liable, nor is he/she liable in tort.

Reasonable Belief
✓ The facts or circumstances that an individual knows, or should know, are such as to cause an ordinary and prudent person to act or think in a similar way under similar circumstances.

Deadly Force
✓ Deadly force: Any use of force that is likely to cause death or serious bodily harm.

✓ Force that is likely or intended to cause death or great bodily harm; may be reasonable or unreasonable, depending on the circumstances.

Excessive Force
✓ That amount of force which is beyond the need and circumstances of the particular event or which is not justified in the light of all the circumstances as in the case of deadly force to protect property as contrasted with protecting life.

Dangerous & Deadly Weapons
✓ Dangerous Weapons: Any device or instrument which, in the manner it is used or intended to be used, is calculated or likely to produce death or great bodily harm.

✓ Deadly Weapons: Any firearm, whether loaded or unloaded; or device designed as a weapon and capable of producing death or great bodily harm.

Levels of Force Continuum

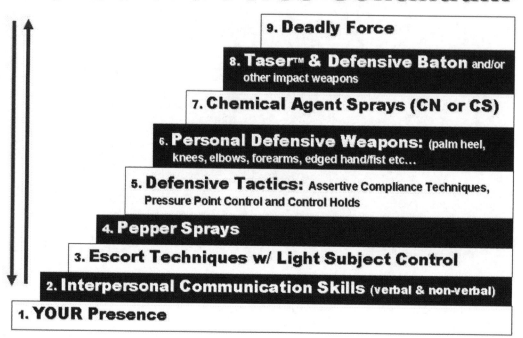

Levels of a Force Continuum

9. **Deadly Force**

8. **Taser™ & Defensive Baton** and/or other impact weapons

7. **Chemical Agent Sprays (CN or CS)**

6. **Personal Defensive Weapons:** (palm heel, knees, elbows, forearms, edged hand/fist etc...

5. **Defensive Tactics:** Assertive Compliance Techniques, Pressure Point Control and Control Holds

4. **Pepper Sprays**

3. **Escort Techniques w/ Light Subject Control**

2. **Interpersonal Communication Skills** (verbal & non-verbal)

1. **YOUR Presence**

A use of force continuum is a standard that provides law enforcement officials & security personnel (such as police officers, probation officers, or corrections officers) with guidelines as to how much force may be used against a resisting subject in a given situation. In certain ways it is similar to the military rules of engagement. The purpose of these models is to clarify, for both officers and citizens, the complex subject of use of force by law officers.

Although various criminal justice agencies have developed different models of the continuum, there is no universal standard model.

The first examples of use of force continua were developed in the 1980s and early 1990s. Early models were depicted in various formats, including graphs, semicircular "gauges", and linear progressions.

Most often the models are presented in "stair step" fashion, with each level of force matched by a corresponding level of subject resistance, although it is generally noted that an officer need not progress through each level before reaching the final level of force. These progressions rest on the premise that officers should escalate and de-escalate their level of force in response to the subject's actions.

Although the use of force continuum is used primarily as a training tool for law officers, it is also valuable with civilians, such as in criminal trials or hearings by police review boards. In particular, a graphical representation of a use of force continuum is useful to a jury when deciding whether an officer's use of force was reasonable.

Subjects Actions – Officer's Actions

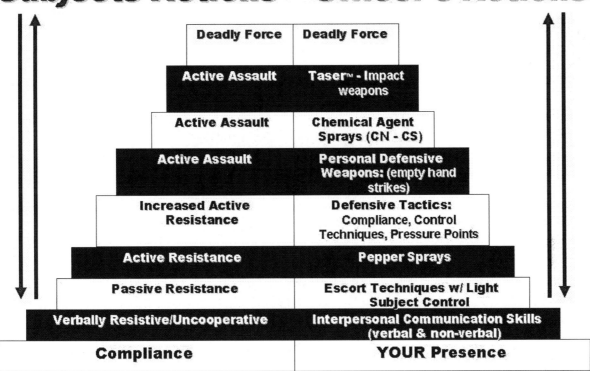

Subjects Actions – Officer's Actions

Deadly Force	Deadly Force
Active Assault	Taser™ - Impact weapons
Active Assault	Chemical Agent Sprays (CN - CS)
Active Assault	Personal Defensive Weapons: (empty hand strikes)
Increased Active Resistance	Defensive Tactics: Compliance, Control Techniques, Pressure Points
Active Resistance	Pepper Sprays
Passive Resistance	Escort Techniques w/ Light Subject Control
Verbally Resistive/Uncooperative	Interpersonal Communication Skills (verbal & non-verbal)
Compliance	YOUR Presence

Copyright © Personal Safety Training Inc. Defense Tactics System™

Lawful Use of Force is permissible:
1. When used to effect an arrest
2. When used to overcome resistance
3. When used to prevent escape
4. When used in self-defense
5. When used in the defense of others

Use of Force **MUST** be Reasonable. YOU should always take into consideration the <u>facts</u> and the <u>circumstances</u> of the incident.
✓ Type of crime and severity of the crime
✓ Resistance of the subject during the arrest or when needing to control them
✓ The threat and safety to others in the area

Subject and Officer Factors

Many factors may affect your selection of an appropriate level of force/control. These factors should be articulated in your post incident documentation.

Examples may include:

- **Age**

  In dealing with a subject who is agile, younger, faster, stronger, and has more stamina an older officer may have to use more force/control. In contrast a younger officer would use less control/force on an older person.

- **Size**

  In dealing with a larger subject, a smaller officer may need to use more force to control the subject. A larger officer would obviously, use less force to control a subject who is smaller.

- **Skill Level**

  In dealing with a subject who is skilled in mixed martial arts or an expert in karate, it may be more difficult to control them based on their skill level. An officer who is skilled in defensive tactics, may only need to use a minimum of force (with proper technique) to control a subject. An officer without current training and experience may need to use more force to control a subject.

- **Relative Strength**

  The different body composition of males and females may be a factor in controlling a member of the opposite gender. Females typically have less torso strength than their male counterparts. A male officer may have to use less force to control a female subject. Whereas, a female officer may need to use more force to control a male subject.

- **Multiple Aggressors**

  An officer who is being physically attacked by multiple aggressors is at a disadvantage. Even a highly skilled officer in defensive tactics is likely to be harmed in a situation such as this. In order to survive multiple aggressor attacks, higher levels of force may be necessary.

Increasing the Level of Force

Certain circumstances may cause the officer to increase the level of force. These factors should be articulated in your post incident documentation.

Examples may include:

- **Disability:** Officers who are disabled may find it necessary to increase the level of force to control a subject or to defend against an attack.

- **Ground Situations:** If you are on the ground with a subject and you do not have control of them, you are at a disadvantage. Officers face a high risk of injury when not in control of a subject on the ground. You are also at a high risk of danger if you are on the ground and the subject is standing. Today, the popularity of mixed martial arts (MMA) can be a real threat to officers. The common vernacular with MMA is "the ground and pound". Officers must realize this and know that an increased level of force may be needed to survive a ground situation.

- **Special Knowledge:** When an officer has encountered a subject who they have had previous contact with, and knows the person's potential for combat, or that they are prone to carrying weapons. The officer may need to approach the situation with the intent to increase the force rapidly if needed. Special knowledge may include: martial arts back ground, propensity for using/carrying weapons, arrests, etc...

- **Injury or Exhaustion:** If an officer is injured during a situation, the officer may need to increase the level of force to end the situation or bring it under control. Exhaustion is also an important factor. Having to physically control an individual for a prolonged length of time will rapidly fatigue an officer. An increased level of force may be needed to end the situation. .

- **Proximity to the Officer's Defensive Tools:** When an officer's defensive tool is taken from them, injury and even death may be imminent. Officers may need to escalate rapidly through the levels of force to survive this type of situation. The defensive tools that can be taken and used against an officer may include the following: firearms, chemical sprays, electronic stunning devices, impact weapons, etc.

Vulnerable Areas of the Body: Low Risk Target Areas

Knowledge of defense tactics is very important, but just as important is where and when you would deploy your defensive tactics if/when necessary.* Without this knowledge and understanding, your interventions could be ineffective or expose you to unnecessary liability risk.

The "Vulnerable Areas" of the body diagrams denote lower, medium, and high-risk target areas.

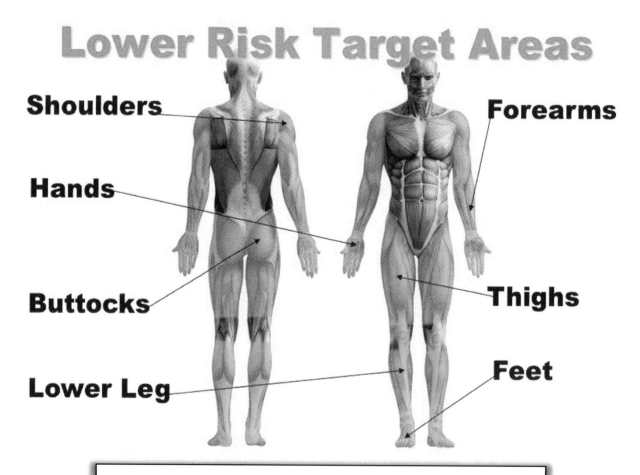

Lower Risk Target Areas

Shoulders

Hands

Buttocks

Lower Leg

Forearms

Thighs

Feet

> **Low Risk Target Areas are for situations where the subject is resisting/attacking an officer or another person.**

The subject's body would be considered low risk for the application of blocks and restraint techniques (excluding the Head, Neck and Spine).

The level of resultant trauma to these areas tends to be minimal or temporary, yet exceptions may occur.

* An individual/agency MUST always consider their policies and procedures, state and federal laws when using any force or self-defense interventions.

Vulnerable Areas of the Body: Medium Risk Target Areas

Knowledge of defense tactics is very important, but just as important is where and when you would deploy your defensive tactics if/when necessary.* Without this knowledge and understanding, your interventions could be ineffective or expose you to unnecessary liability risk.

The "Vulnerable Areas" of the body diagrams denote lower, medium, and high-risk target areas.

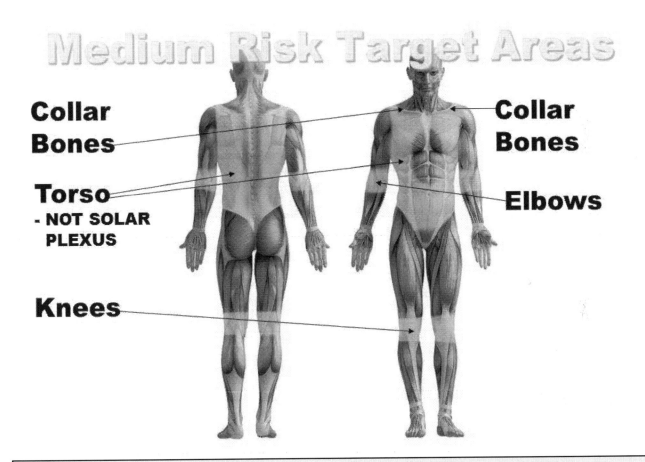

Collar Bones

Torso
- NOT SOLAR PLEXUS

Knees

Collar Bones

Elbows

Medium Risk Target Areas are for situations where the subject is resisting/attacking an officer or when force applied to a Low Risk Target Area fails to overcome the subject's resistance/attack.*

Medium Risk Targets are areas of the human body that include joints and areas that are in close proximity to a High Risk Target Area. Risk of potential injury is increased.

The level of resultant trauma to these areas tends to be moderate to serious. Injury may last for longer periods of time, or may be temporary.

* An individual/agency MUST always consider their policies and procedures, state and federal laws when using any force or self-defense interventions.

Vulnerable Areas of the Body: High Risk Target Areas

Knowledge of defense tactics is very important, but just as important is where and when you would deploy your defensive tactics if/when necessary.*
Without this knowledge and understanding, your interventions could be ineffective or expose you to unnecessary liability risk.

The "Vulnerable Areas" of the body diagrams denote lower, medium, and high-risk target areas.

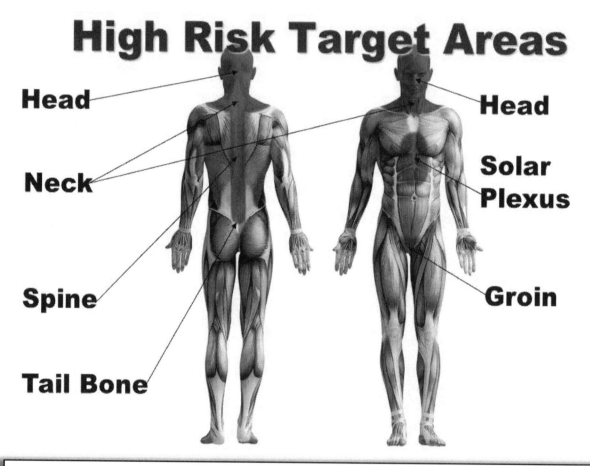

High Risk Target Areas

Head

Neck

Spine

Tail Bone

Head

Solar
Plexus

Groin

High Risk Target Areas are for situations where the subject is using force that is likely to cause serious injury or death to an officer or another person.*

Force directed to High Risk Target Areas may cause greater risk of injury to the subject. Officers must be justified and reasonable in using deadly force against a subject.

The level of resultant trauma to these areas tends to be serious and/or long lasting. Injury to subject may include serious bodily injury, unconsciousness, shock or death.

* An individual/agency MUST always consider their policies and procedures, state and federal laws when using any force or self-defense interventions.

Module Two –Defensive Tactics Fundamentals

The defensive tactics fundamentals are the basis of the Defense Tactics System™ training program. Without proper understanding and execution of the fundamentals the techniques will be ineffective and useless. Below is the definition of fundamental.

Fundamentals

Fun·da·men·tal
(from the Latin medieval: *fundāmentālis*: belonging to a foundation. 1400-50, late Middle English.
—*Synonyms* 1. Indispensable, primary.

–adjective
1. Serving as, or being an essential part of, a foundation or basis; basic; underlying: *fundamental principles; the fundamental structure.*
2. Of, pertaining to, or affecting the foundation or basis: *a fundamental revision.*
3. Being an original or primary source: *a fundamental idea.*

–noun

1. A basic principle, rule, law, or the like, that serves as the groundwork of a system; essential part: *to master the fundamentals of a trade.*
2. Also called fundamental note, fundamental tone. *Music.*
3. *The* root of a chord.
4. The generator of a series of harmonics.
5. *Physics,* The component of lowest frequency in a composite wave.

Defensive Tactics Fundamentals

- Stance-Balance-Stability
- Defensive Movements
- Core Energy Principle
- Defense Verbalization
- Distraction Techniques
- Escape Strategies
- Reactionary Gap
- Hand Positions

The Bladed (defensive) Stance

The Bladed (defensive) Stance

> All techniques in the defense tactics training are performed from the bladed stance.

Objective

> Demonstrate how to correctly position your body to protect your vulnerable line and maintain stance, balance and stability.

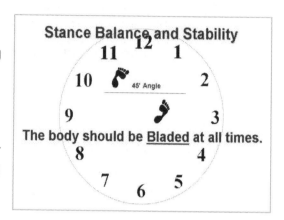

Performance—Bladed Stance

> Face the clock (diagram on PowerPoint or imagine a clock in front of you) with your feet shoulder-width apart.

1. Step straight back with either left or right foot. Usually individuals prefer to have their dominant foot to the rear.

2. If you stepped back with your right foot, turn your feet and body to the one o'clock position.

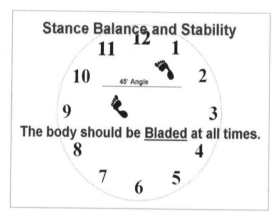

3. If you stepped forward with your left foot, turn your feet and body to the eleven o'clock position.

4. Keep your weight equal on both feet, and your knees slightly bent.

Performance Stability Test (Bladed Stance)

1. Partner exercise (A & B)

2. Partner A places his/her feet together. Partner B gently pushes partner A to the front, back, left side and right side. Reverse roles.

3. Partner A stands with his/her feet should width apart. Partner B gently pushes partner A to the front, back, left side and right side. Reverse roles.

4. Partner A now assumes the bladed stance. Partner B gently pushes partner A to the front, back, left side and right side. Reverse roles.

The Bladed Stance protects your "Vulnerable Line" away from the subject.

Defensive Movements: Forward Shuffle

Forward movement is used to engage a subject for control or defense.

Forward Shuffle

This Defensive movement involves being able to move forward while maintaining balance and stability. All defensive tactics techniques are enhanced with defensive movement.

Objective

Demonstrate how to correctly move forward.

Performance—Forward Movement

1. Assume the bladed stance.
2. Take a short step forward with your front foot (shuffle).
3. Follow up with a short step forward using your rear foot.
4. Continue forward, using forward shuffling movement.

Caution: If the feet come together, balance and stability are compromised (common mistake).

The rule of defensive movement is:
The foot that is closest to the direction you want to go, always moves first.

Defensive Movements: Rear Shuffle

Rear movement is used to disengage from an aggressor.

Rear Shuffle
This Defensive movement involves being able to move to the rear (backwards) while maintaining balance and stability. All defensive tactics techniques are enhanced with defensive movement.

Objective
Demonstrate how to correctly move to the rear.

Performance—Rear Movement
1. Assume the bladed stance.
2. Take a short step to back with the rear foot (shuffle).
3. Follow up with a short step back using your front foot.
4. Continue backwards, using rear shuffling movement.

Caution: If the feet come together, balance and stability are compromised (common mistake).

Caution: Back pedaling is another common mistake.

Caution: Obstacles in your environment.

The rule of defensive movement is:
The foot that is closest to the direction you want to go, always moves first.

Defensive Movements: Side to Side Shuffle

Side to side movement is used to avoid an attack from an aggressor.

Side to Side Shuffle
This Defensive movement involves being able to move side to side while maintaining balance and stability. All defensive tactics techniques are enhanced with defensive movement.

Objective
Demonstrate how to correctly move side to side

Performance—Side-to-Side Movement

1. Assume the bladed stance.
2. Take a short step to the right using your right foot.
3. Follow up with a short step to the right using your left foot.
4. Take a short step to the left using your left.
5. Follow up with a short step to the left using your right foot.

Caution: If the feet come together, balance and stability are compromised (common mistake).

Caution: Crossing feet up is another common mistake.

Caution: Obstacles in your environment.

The rule of defensive movement is:
The foot that is closest to the direction you want to go, always moves first.

Defensive Movements: Forward and Rear Pivoting

Pivoting is used to reposition or to enhance your energy when using personal defensive weapons or defensive control tactics

Forward & Rear Pivoting
This Defensive movement involves being able to pivot forward or back while maintaining balance and stability. All defensive tactics techniques are enhanced with defensive movement.

Objective
Demonstrate how to correctly pivot forward and backward.

Performance—Pivoting (forward and back)
1. Assume the bladed stance.
2. Take an arcing step forward with your rear foot (forward pivot).
3. Take an arcing step backward with your front foot (rear pivot).
4. When pivoting forward or backward, always remain balanced and stable.
5. Pivots can be small movements or up to a 360 degree pivot.

Caution: If the feet come together, balance and stability are compromised (common mistake).

Caution: Crossing feet up is another common mistake.

Caution: Obstacles in your environment.

Robot Exercise (The Best Self-Defense Technique!)

Defensive Movement "Robot Exercise"

The robot exercise involves being able to move in a lateral motion (side to side) to avoid an attack that us coming at you from a distance of 4' away or greater.

Objective

Demonstrate how to correctively avoid a forward attack by moving out of the way.

Performance—Robot Exercise

1. Defender assumes a bladed defensive stance.
2. From 4-6" away the attacker places hands out directly toward the defender.
3. Attacker moves forward toward the defender, attempting to gently touch either shoulder of the defender.
4. Defender waits for last moment to move to either side away from attack.
5. Using sounds and/or movements will assist defender in distracting the attacker.
6. Once out of the attack zone, defender can proceed to keep moving away from the attacker.

Caution: Do not move too late!

Caution: Do not move too soon or attacker will have time to adjust (reaction time) and follow/track you.

Caution: Crossing feet up is another common mistake.

Caution: Beware of obstacles in your environment.

Core Energy Principle

Core Energy

Our central and most essential part of our strength and power is our core energy. Without core energy we rely on our extremities which are not as strong as our central core. All defensive tactics techniques utilize this essential principle.

Having Core Energy will:

✓ Give YOU advantage over subjects.
✓ Provide YOU power for counter blocks/defenses.
✓ Help the YOU better control and decentralize a physically resistive subject.

Objective

Demonstrate how to correctly use your core energy.

Performance—Core Energy

1. Partner exercise (A & B)

2. Partner A faces partner B with his/her elbows away from their core.

3. Partner B moves forward toward partner A. Partner A pushes partner B back by pushing at their shoulders. How did it go? Reverse roles.

4. Partner A again, faces partner B with his/her elbows down towards their core.

Partner B moves forward toward partner A. Partner A pushes partner B back by pushing at their shoulders. How did it go? Reverse roles

Defensive Verbalization

During all Defenses: Use loud repetitive Defensive Verbalizations

- ➢ NO!
- ➢ STOP!
- ➢ GET BACK!
- ➢ STOP RESISTING!
- ➢ BREAK YOUR FALL!
- ➢ WERE GOING DOWN ONTO THE GROUND!

Defensive Verbalization:
Creates witnesses
Establishes authority
Keeps YOU breathing
May be used a distraction
Alerts other of a confrontation
Provides direction to the aggressor
Mitigates liability risk to YOU and your agency

The Art of Distraction

Is a process by which we buy valuable time to **Escape, Defend** or **Control.**

Sounds (Loud Scream/Yell) - Movements – Psychological - Lights

Distractions affect the senses which take time for the mind to process the new information. They mainly affect a person's sight and sense of hearing; however, psychological distractions such as asking a person something completely out of the ordinary can cause a mental delay as well. Distractions have been used since ancient times. A valuable advantage!

Sounds: Using a loud scream or yell can cause a momentary delay.

Movements: Using your hands, eyes, and body can distract and cause a momentary delay.

Psychological: Asking a person something completely out of the ordinary can cause them a mental delay.

Lights: Flashlights, the sun, emergency lights, etc., can cause a delay.

Escape Strategies

Escape Strategies

- Escape is the act or instance of breaking free from danger or threat, or from being trapped, restrained, confined or isolated against your will.
- Planning is the cognitive process of thinking about what you will do in the event of something happening.

Reactionary Gap

The Reactionary Gap is 4-6 Feet. "Action beats Reaction with-in the Reactionary Gap"
The distance between and individual and an agressoe in which the ability to react is impaired due to the close proximity of the agressor.

Hand Positions

There are six basic hand positions.

Objective

Demonstrate how to correctly use your hands in the stop, caution, defensive, authoritative, directive and open positions.

Performance—<u>Stop or Caution</u> Hand Positions

1. Assume the bladed stance
2. Position your arms with your elbows down and you palms facing outward.
3. The non-verbal message says "don't come close to me," or a non-threatening message if you are moving forward.

Performance—<u>Defensive or Authoritative</u> Hand Positions

1. Assume the bladed stance
2. Position your arms with your elbows down and you palms in a bladed position.
3. Position your arms with your elbows down and your palms down.
3. The nonverbal message is defensive or authority.

- **Caution:** Closing your hands into a fist position may send a message of aggression.

Performance—<u>Directive or Open</u> Hand Positions

1. Assume the bladed Stance
2. Position your arms and hands pointing with your hand in the direction you want someone to go.
3. Position your arms with your elbows down and you palms facing upward.

- **Caution:** Do not point when giving directions, as pointing is perceived as a derogatory gesture.

Module Three – Contact and Cover Positioning

Initial Contact Front (1 Person)

Initial Contact (1 person)

Is a technique that teaches individuals how to safely approach a subject and make initial contact.

Objective

Demonstrate how to safely approach a subject while moving forward with defensive movement to make physical contact.

Note: A two person Initial Contact is safer as you have controlled both arms of the aggressor.

Note: This technique can be done to the front or behind the subject. It is safer to perform from behind the subject.

Performance—Initial Contact (1 person)

1. Move forward towards subject at a 45-degree angle.

2. Use defensive movement and keep your hands in the caution position.

3. Your body should be bladed away (vulnerable line) from the subject. Left side forward on left side of subject and right side forward on right side of subject.

4. Firmly capture the elbow of the subject with both hands (thumbs up).

5. Bring your shoulder slightly forward to further protect your vulnerable line if you are in front of the subject. Avoid this if you are behind the subject.

Caution: Armed individuals should keep gun side back and away from the subject regardless of their approaching side.

Caution: Approaching a subject to the front is more dangerous for the individual than approaching from behind.

Initial Contact Front (2 Person)

Initial Contact (2 person)
Is a technique that teaches individuals how to safely approach a subject and make contact.

Objective
Demonstrate how to safely approach a subject while moving forward with defensive movement to make physical contact.

Note: A two person Initial Contact is safer as you have controlled both arms of the aggressor

Note: This technique can be done to the front or behind the subject. It is safer to perform from behind the subject.

Performance—Initial Contact (2 person)
1. Move forward towards subject at a 45-degree angle.
2. Use defensive movement and keep your hands in the caution position.
3. Your body should be bladed away (vulnerable line) from the subject. Left side forward on left of subject and right side forward on right side of subject.
4. Firmly capture the elbow of the subject with both hands (thumbs up).
5. Bring your shoulder slightly forward to further protect your vulnerable line if you are in front of the subject. Avoid this if you are behind the subject.

Caution: Armed individuals should keep gun side back and away from the subject regardless of their approaching side.

Caution: Approaching a subject to the front is more dangerous for the individuals than approaching from behind.

Initial Contact Rear (1 Person)

Initial Contact (1 person)

Is a technique that teaches individuals how to safely approach a subject and make initial contact.

Objective

Demonstrate how to safely approach a subject while moving forward with defensive movement to make physical contact.

Note: A two person Initial Contact is safer as you have controlled both arms of the aggressor.

Note: This technique can be done to the front or behind the subject. It is safer to perform from behind the subject.

Performance—Initial Contact (1 person)

1. Move forward towards subject at a 45-degree angle.

2. Use defensive movement and keep your hands in the caution position.

3. Your body can be (but not necessary) bladed away (vulnerable line) from the subject. Left side forward on left of subject and right side forward on right side of subject.

4. Firmly capture the elbow of the subject with both hands (thumbs up).

Caution: Armed individuals should keep gun side back and away from the subject regardless of their approaching side.

Caution: Approaching a subject to the front is more dangerous for the individual than approaching from behind.

Initial Contact Rear (2 Person)

Initial Contact (2 person)
Is a technique that teaches individuals how to safely approach a subject and make contact.

Objective
Demonstrate how to safely approach a subject while moving forward with defensive movement to make physical contact.

Note: A two person Initial Contact is safer as you have controlled both arms of the aggressor

Note: This technique can be done to the front or behind the subject. It is safer to perform from behind the subject.

Performance—Initial Contact (1 or 2 person)

1. Move forward towards subject at a 45-degree angle.
2. Use defensive movement and keep your hands in the caution position.
3. Your body can be (but not necessary) bladed away (vulnerable line) from the subject. Left side forward on left of subject and right side forward on right side of subject.
4. Firmly capture the elbow of the subject with both hands (thumbs up).

Caution: Armed individuals should keep gun side back and away from the subject regardless of their approaching side.

Caution: Approaching a subject to the front is more dangerous for the individuals than approaching from behind.

Contact and Cover Positioning

Contact and Cover (Team Positioning) is the main strategy for the Healthcare Defensive Tactics System. Contact and Cover techniques are used by individuals during situations where they are dealing with a subject(s). The purpose of the technique is to deter a situation from getting out of control and to improve the individual's safety by having other individuals in a constant state of preparation to act in the event that the situation gets out of control.

Contact (Team Leader)
The contact individual is the focal point for the subject as this individual is the primary communicator giving directions to the subject. In many situations the contact individual(s) will initiate communications.

In the pictures the contact individual is communicating with subject which may act as a distraction, allowing cover individuals (team members) to move in and gain physical control if needed. The contact individual should have a prearranged "cue" (verbal or non-verbal) alerting the cover individuals to initiate physical control.

Cover (Team Members)
The cover individual(s) role is to watch subject(s) for any attempt to flee or assault the contact individual. The cover individual(s) should be ever vigilant and ready to respond, and alert the contact individual of suspicious activity or an imminent attempt to assault the contact individual.

Special Note: Cover individuals should maintain their distance (stay back) until needed (see top picture). Moving in too soon may cause subject to feel as though he/she is being corned.

Contact and Cover should be used for all situations involving subjects and witnesses.

Module Four – Escort Strategies and Techniques

Escort Strategies and Techniques (1 Person)

Escort Technique (1 person)
Is a technique that teaches individuals how to safely escort a cooperative subject.

Objective
Demonstrate how to safely escort a cooperative subject using proper distancing, verbal communications and non-verbal communication.

Performance—Escort Technique (1 person)

1. Maintain a 45-degree angle and distance of (4-6 feet) behind the individual.
2. Direct subject where you want them to go
3. Use proper verbal and non-verbal skills.
4. Do not point, use open hand gestures.
5. Maintain Awareness.

Caution: If subject stops and moves towards you, use verbal and non-verbal communication and defensive movements.

Escort Strategies and Techniques (2 Person)

Escort Technique (2 person)

Is a technique that teaches individuals how to safely escort a cooperative subject.

Objective

Demonstrate how to safely escort a cooperative subject using proper distancing, verbal communications and non-verbal communication.

Performance—Escort Technique (2 person)

1. Maintain a 45-degree angle and distance of 4-6 feet behind the individual.
2. Direct subject where you want them to go.
3. Use proper verbal and non-verbal skills.
4. Do not point, use open hand gestures.
5. Maintain Awareness.

Caution: If subject stops and moves towards you, use verbal and non-verbal communication and defensive movements.

Hands-On Escort Technique (1 Person)

Hands-On Escort Technique (1 person)
Is a technique that teaches an individual how to escort a subject using light subject control.

Objective
Demonstrate how to safely escort a passive resistive subject using light subject control with proper hand and body positioning.

Performance—Hands-On Escort (1 person)

1. From the initial contact position.
2. If you are on the right side of the subject your right hand slides down and grips the wrist. Same for left side.
3. Bring the subjects gripped wrist to the side of your body (holstered position).
4. The subjects palm should be facing upward and above any defensive tools you may be carrying.
5. Maintain a 45-degree angle behind the subject and escort them to the desired location.

Caution: When gripping the appropriate wrist, the web of your hand should be on the ulna side of the subject's wrist. This ensures that there core strength is eliminated due to proper positioning.

Caution: When initiating the hands-on escort and when moving the subject, remember to stay at a 45-degree angle behind the subject.

Hands-On Escort Technique (2 Person)

Hands-On Escort Technique (2 person)
Is a technique that teaches individuals how to escort a subject using light subject control.

Objective
Demonstrate how to safely escort a passive resistive subject using light subject control with proper hand and body positioning.

Performance—Hands-On Escort (2 person)

1. From the initial contact position.

2. The individual on the right side of the subject will slide their right hand down and grip the wrist. Same for left side.

3. Bring the subjects gripped wrist to the side of your body (holstered position).

4. The subjects palm should be facing upward and above any defensive tools you may be carrying.

5. Maintain a 45-degree angle behind the subject and escort them to the desired location.

Caution: When gripping the appropriate wrist, the web of your hand should be on the ulna side of the subject's wrist. This ensures that there core strength is eliminated due to proper positioning.

Caution: When initiating the hands-on escort and when moving the subject, remember to stay at a 45-degree angle behind the subject.

Caution: Both individuals acting with the same timing and control can reduce the possibility of escalation.

Module Five – Control and Decentralization Techniques

Control and Decentralization Techniques— One Arm Take-Down

One Arm Take-Down (part 1)
Is a technique that teaches an individual how decentralize a resistive subject using a take-down control technique.

Objective
Demonstrate how to control a subject using a one-bar take-down for a subject who is actively resisting.

Performance—One Arm Take-Down (part 1)

1. From the hands-on escort position.

2. The individual will place their wrist onto the tricep of the subject (2 -3" above the elbow).

3. The individual will then apply pressure to the tricep while moving forward or pivoting to the rear.

4. Use loud defensive verbalizations (NO, STOP, STOP RESISTING, WERE GOING DOWN, BREAK YOUR FALL, to direct the aggressor to stop resisting you and to direct them down.

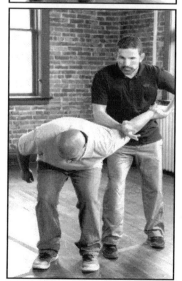

Caution: Be aware of your environment and what direction you are moving the resistive subject towards.

Control and Decentralization Techniques: One Arm Take-Down—Part Two

One Arm Take-Down (part 2)
Is a technique that teaches an individual how decentralize a resistive subject using a take-down control technique.

Objective
Demonstrate how to control a subject using a one-arm take-down for a subject who is actively resisting.

Performance— One Arm Take-Down (part 2)

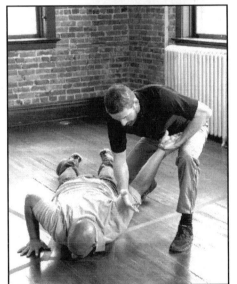

5. Continue to use movement and pressure on the tricep to direct the aggressor to the ground.

6. Use loud defensive verbalizations (NO, STOP, STOP RESISTING, WERE GOING DOWN, BREAK YOUR FALL, to direct the aggressor to stop resisting you and direct them down.

Caution: Be aware of your environment and what direction you are moving the resistive subject towards.

Caution: The prone position is a temporary position which may predispose the subject to breathing difficulties.

Continuously monitor subject and seek medical attention if needed.

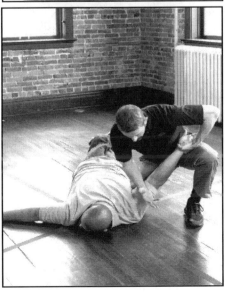

Prone Control Positions

Prone Position Caution

- Individuals in a prone position may have difficulty breathing.
- Monitor individuals and place them on their side, seated position or get them up as soon as possible.

Prone Control is a temporary position!

Positional asphyxia

Positional asphyxia is a form of asphyxia which occurs when someone's position prevents them from breathing adequately. A small but significant number of people die suddenly and without apparent reason during restraint by police, prison (corrections) officers and health care staff. Positional asphyxia may be a factor in some of these deaths.

Research has suggested that restraining a person in a face down position is likely to cause greater restriction of breathing than restraining a person face up.

Many law enforcement and health personnel are now taught to avoid restraining people face down or to do so only for a very short period of time.

Prone Control is a temporary position!

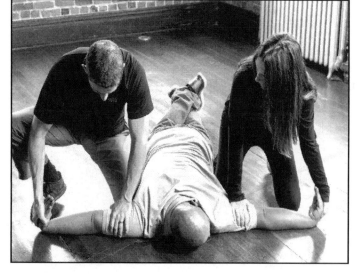

Rear Arm Control Technique

Rear Arm Control Technique (part 1)
Is a technique that teaches an individual how to control a resistive subject from the escort technique.

Objective
Demonstrate how to control a resistive subject using the rear arm control technique from the hands-on escort position.

Performance—Rear Arm Control Technique (part 1)

1. From the hands-on escort position.
2. The subject becomes resistive by pushing their arm backward.
3. The individual moves with the resistance and repositions him/herself turning 90 degree towards the aggressor.
4. The individual pulls the resistive subjects arm into his/her core.
5. Use loud defensive verbalizations (NO, STOP, STOP RESISTING, to direct the aggressor to stop resisting you.

Caution: Tuck your head into the shoulder of the aggressor. This will prevent the aggressor from striking you with a rear head butt.

Rear Arm Control Technique

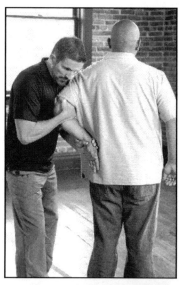

Rear Arm Control Technique (part 2)
Is a technique that teaches an individual how to control a resistive subject from the escort technique.

Objective
Demonstrate how to control a resistive subject using the rear arm control technique from the hands-on escort position.

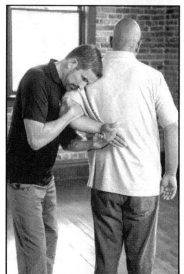

Performance—Rear Arm Control Technique (part 2)

6. Continue to control the arm in your core by pulling it into you.
7. Reposition your hand on the wrist; bring your fingertips onto the resistive subject's knuckles.
8. Gently bring the subject's arm upward into their lower back as you bring the subject's fingertips towards you.
9. Use loud defensive verbalizations (NO, STOP, STOP RESISTING, to direct the aggressor to stop resisting you.

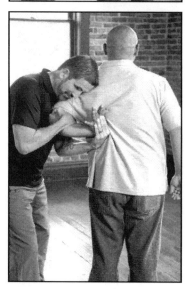

From the rear arm control you can:

- Escort the subject
- Handcuff the subject

Caution: Tuck your head into the shoulder of the resistive subject. This will prevent the subject from striking you with a rear head butt.

Module Six - Handcuffing Techniques

The Healthcare Defensive Tactics System™ handcuffing techniques can be used with either chain or hinged handcuffs.

The Chain Handcuffs are held in a pistol grip position allowing the single bars to rotate through completely.

Handcuffing Stance (Chain Cuffs)

The Hinged Handcuffs are held in a modified pistol grip allowing the single bars to rotate through completely.

Handcuffing Stance (Hinged Cuffs)

Handcuff Nomenclature

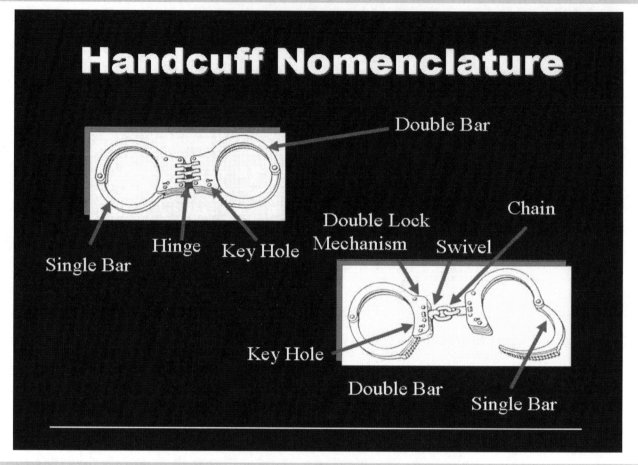

General Handcuffing Guidelines

- **Handcuff behind the back:** exceptions- injuries, deformities, pregnant etc.
- **Make sure Handcuffs are properly fitted:** NOT to loose and NOT to tight.
- **Never underestimate a Subject:** subjects can fight, injure, subdue and incapacitate officers.
- **Double Lock Handcuffs:** For the safety of officer, subject and public.
- **Position-Stability-Awareness:** Maintain a balanced stance at a 45-degree angle behind the subject and stay aware at all times.
- **Search after Handcuffing:** Searching prior to handcuffing can be dangerous.
- **Handcuffs should be applied quickly:** physical resistance can occur during the handcuffing process. Cuff as quickly and smoothly as possible.
- **Before-During-After Handcuffing:** awareness of subject, environment and possible accomplices should never cease.
- **All subjects arrested should be Handcuffed:** follow agency procedures for arrests and detentions.
- **Multiple Handcuffs:** more than one pair of cuffs may be needed for handcuffing a large person.

Standing Handcuffing Technique (part 1)

Is a technique that teaches officers how to handcuff a subject who is cooperative or semi-cooperative in a standing position.

Objective: Demonstrate how to position, approach and safely handcuff a cooperative or semi-cooperative subject who is in a standing position.

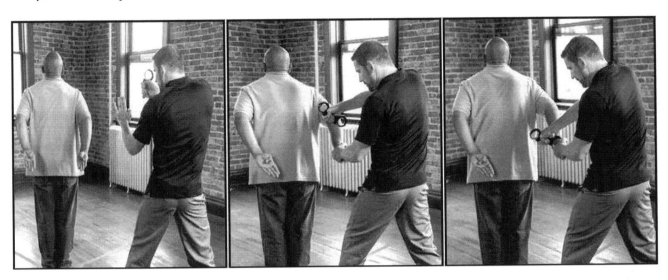

Performance
Standing Handcuffing Technique (part 1)

1. Before entering into the reactionary gap, position the subject facing away from you and looking upward.
2. The subject should have their hands-behind them away from their body.
3. The feet of the subject can be together or separated. Follow agency guidelines.
4. Approach at a 45-degree angle using defensive movement.
5. With your control hand, grip the subject's hand using a reverse handshake.
6. Place the bottom cuff onto the thumb side (radial) of the subject's wrist.
7. Maintain position and stay aware.

Caution: Most resistance occurs after the first cuff has been applied. Maintain awareness and be prepared to escape or utilize a decentralizing technique if needed.

Standing Handcuffing Technique (part 2)

Is a technique that teaches officers how to handcuff a subject who is cooperative or semi-cooperative in a standing position.

Objective: Demonstrate how to position, approach and safely handcuff a cooperative or semi-cooperative subject who is in a standing position.

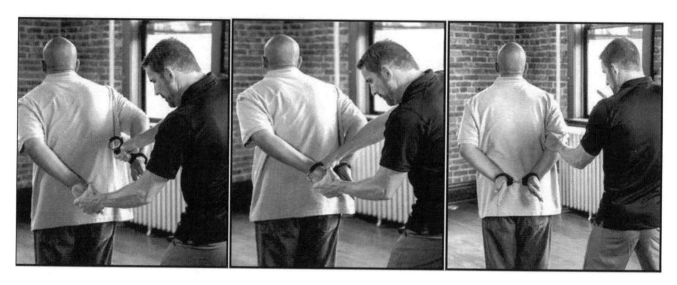

Performance
Standing Handcuffing Technique (part 2)

8. After first cuff is applied, release your control hand and grip the subject's free hand using a handshake position.
9. Bring the top cuff over and cuff the thumb side (radial) of the wrist.
10. Check for proper fit and position of both handcuffed wrists. Adjust if needed.
11. Double lock handcuffs.

Caution: Most resistance occurs after the first cuff has been applied. Maintain awareness and be prepared to escape or utilize a decentralizing technique if needed.

~ Follow agency policy and procedure for searching the subject.

Proper Fit and Placement/Double Locking

- Check for proper fit by pinching your index finger and thumb between the cuffs and the aggressors wrist.

- Handcuffs should be placed on either side of the subject's wrist.

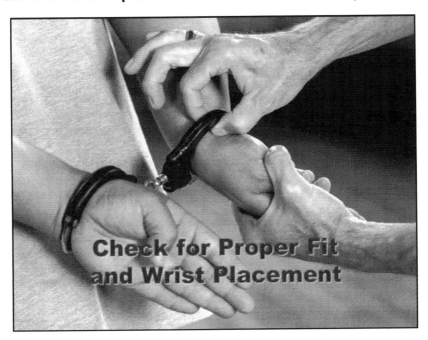

- When placed above the wrists, injuries can occur.

- Double lock the cuffs for the safety of the subject and the officer.

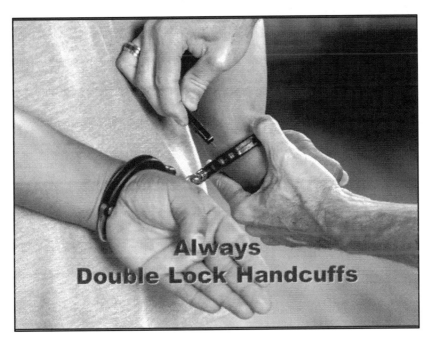

Kneeling Handcuffing Technique (part 1)

Is a technique that teaches officers how to handcuff a subject who is cooperative, semi-cooperative or uncooperative in a kneeling position.

Objective: Demonstrate how to position, approach and safely handcuff a cooperative, semi-cooperative, or an uncooperative subject who is in a kneeling position.

Performance
Kneeling Handcuffing Technique (part 1)

1. Before entering into the reactionary gap, position the subject facing away from you and looking upward.
2. The subject should have their hands-behind them away from their body.
3. The feet of the subject can be together or crossed.
   Follow agency guidelines.
4. Approach at a 45-degree angle using defensive movement.
5. With your control hand, grip the subject's hand using a reverse handshake.
6. Place the bottom cuff onto the thumb side (radial) of the subject's wrist.
7. Maintain position and stay aware.

Caution: Most resistance occurs after the first cuff has been applied. Maintain awareness and be prepared to escape or utilize a decentralizing technique if needed.

Kneeling Handcuffing Technique (part 2)

Is a technique that teaches officers how to handcuff a subject who is cooperative, semi-cooperative or uncooperative in a kneeling position.

Objective: Demonstrate how to position, approach and safely handcuff a cooperative, semi-cooperative, or an uncooperative subject who is in a kneeling position.

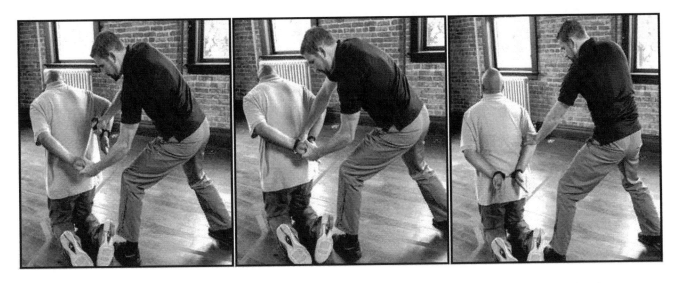

Performance
Kneeling Handcuffing Technique (part 2)

8. After first cuff is applied, release your control hand and grip the subject's free hand using a hand shake position.
9. Bring the top cuff over and cuff the thumb side (radial) of the wrist.
10. Check for proper fit and position of both handcuffed wrists. Adjust if needed.
11. Double lock handcuffs.

Caution: Most resistance occurs after the first cuff has been applied. Maintain awareness and be prepared to escape or utilize a decentralizing technique if needed.

~ Follow agency policy and procedure for searching the subject.

Prone Handcuffing Technique (part 1)

Is a technique that teaches officers how to handcuff a subject who is cooperative, semi-cooperative or uncooperative in a prone position.

Objective: Demonstrate how to position, approach and safely handcuff a cooperative, semi-cooperative, or an uncooperative subject who is in a prone position.

Performance
Prone Handcuffing Technique (part 1)

1. Before entering into the reactionary gap, position the subject facing down and looking away from you.
2. The subject should have their hands/arms out to their side, palms up and raised.
3. The feet of the subject can be together or crossed. Follow agency guidelines.
4. Approach at a 45-degree angle using defensive movement.
5. With your support and strong hand, grip the aggressor hand using a wrist control technique.
6. Step forward with your rear foot towards the head of the subject.
7. Your opposite knee will be positioned on the ground.

Caution: Most resistance occurs after the first cuff has been applied. Maintain awareness and be prepared to escape if needed.

Prone Handcuffing Technique (part 2)

Is a technique that teaches officers how to handcuff a subject who is cooperative, semi-cooperative or uncooperative in a prone position.

Objective: Demonstrate how to position, approach and safely handcuff a cooperative, semi-cooperative, or an uncooperative subject who is in a prone position.

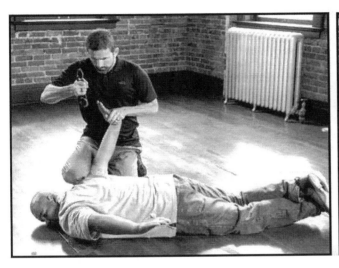 

Performance
Prone Handcuffing Technique (part 2)

8. Position your knee onto the shoulder of the subject.
9. Draw handcuffs into proper position.
10. Place the bottom cuff onto the thumb side (radial) of the subject's wrist.

Caution: Do not place knee onto the head, neck or spine of the subject

Caution: Most resistance occurs after the first cuff has been applied. Maintain awareness and be prepared to escape if needed.

Prone Handcuffing Technique (part 3)

Is a technique that teaches officers how to handcuff a subject who is cooperative, semi-cooperative or uncooperative in a prone position.

Objective: Demonstrate how to position, approach and safely handcuff a cooperative, semi-cooperative, or an uncooperative subject who is in a prone position.

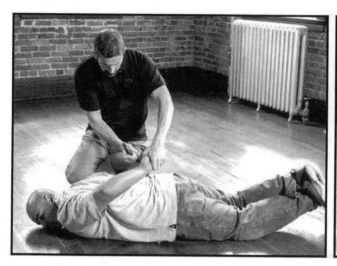 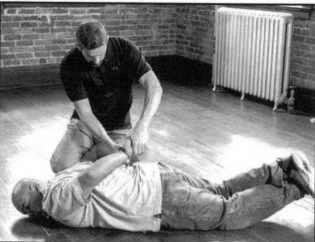

Performance
Prone Handcuffing Technique (part 3)

11. Have the subject place their un-cuffed hand/arm into the middle of their lower back.
12. Bring the subjects cuffed hand/arm down while releasing your hand to grab the un-cuffed hand.
13. Raise the hand of the subject and cuff the thumb side (radial) of the wrist with the top cuff.
14. Check for proper fit and position of both handcuffed wrists. Adjust if needed.
15. Double lock handcuffs.
16. Follow agency policy and procedure for searching the subject.

Caution: Most resistance occurs after the first cuff has been applied. Maintain awareness and be prepared to escape if needed.

~ Follow agency policy and procedure for searching the subject

Standing the Prone Handcuffed Subject (part 1)

Is a technique that teaches officers how to stand a prone handcuffed subject.

Objective: demonstrate how to position and safely stand a handcuffed subject who is in the prone position.

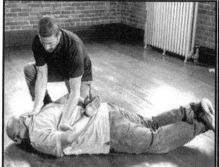  

Performance
Standing the Prone Handcuffed Subject (part 1)

1. Position yourself on the side of the subject with one hand supporting the head and neck (palm up) and your other hand gripping the inside of the elbow (palm up).
2. Using the momentum of the subject, rock them towards you and assist them into a seated position.
3. Once the subject is seated, position yourself on either side of the subject.
4. If on the right side of subject, place your right arm across their shoulder. Same for left side.
5. With your opposite hand grip the elbow, preparing to rock the subject onto their knees.
6. Using the momentum of the subject, rock them and assist them onto their knees.

Caution: Avoid lifting the subject up using your back (muscles) as injuries to officers are highly probable.

Caution: Maintain control of subject when rocking them onto their knees, to avoid the subject falling forward.

Standing the Prone Handcuffed Subject (part 2)

Is a technique that teaches officers how to stand a prone handcuffed subject.

Objective: Demonstrate how to position and safely stand a handcuffed subject who is in the prone position.

Performance
Standing the Prone Handcuffed Subject (part 2)

7. With the subject in the kneeling position, maintain your hand position.
8. Have the subject bring their right foot up in from of them if you are on their right side. Same for left side.
9. Using the momentum of the subject rock them and assist them onto their feet.

Caution: Maintain awareness as subject is now mobile and may be a higher risk to the officer in this position.

Escorting Handcuffed Subject

Personal Safety Training Inc. does not dictate policies or procedures for the use of any arrest, detention, control and restraint, self-defense, use of force or any physical intervention authorized for use by a department/agency or private individual. The suggestions, options and techniques disseminated during this training program are simply that, suggestions, options and techniques. Each individual, department or agency is responsible for developing their own "policies and procedures" regarding use of force, self-defense, physical intervention or physical restraints/control, arrest/detention for their personnel.

Module Seven – Defensive Blocking Techniques

Shoulder Block Defense

Shoulder Block Defense
Is a technique that teaches individuals how to deflect an imminent assault.

Objective
Demonstrate how to properly use a defensive shoulder block against a physical assault to your head.

Performance—Shoulder Block Defense
1. Assume the bladed stance.
2. Bring your chin down.
3. Drop the arm that is in front of you while bringing your shoulder up to your chin.
4. You can slightly rotate your body towards your back side as the assault comes towards you, further deflecting the attack.

During all Defenses:
- Use loud defensive verbalizations (NO, STOP, GET BACK, STOP RESISTING, etc.) to direct the aggressor to stop attacking you.
- Use defensive movements (Escape!)

After all Defenses:
- Follow agency policies and procedures in regard to self-defense.
- Report and Document immediately.

Elbow Block Defense

Elbow Block Defense
Is a technique that teaches individuals how to deflect an imminent assault.

Objective
Demonstrate how to properly use a defensive elbow block against a physical assault to your head.

Performance—Elbow Block Defense
1. Assume the bladed stance.
2. Bring your chin down.
3. Bring your front arm up to your face with your elbow directly in front, creating a shield in front of your face.
4. You can slightly rotate your body towards your back side as the assault comes towards you, further deflecting the attack.

During all Defenses:
- Use loud defensive verbalizations (NO, STOP, GET BACK, STOP RESISTING, etc.) to direct the aggressor to stop attacking you.
- Use defensive movements (Escape!)

After all Defenses:
- Follow agency policies and procedures in regard to self-defense.
- Report and Document immediately.

Turtle Block Defense

Turtle Block Defense
Is a technique that teaches individuals how to deflect an imminent assault.

Objective
Demonstrate how to properly use a defensive turtle block against a physical assault to your head and torso.

Performance—Turtle Block Defense
1. Assume the bladed stance.
2. Bring your chin down.
3. Bring both arms up in front of your face with your elbows directly in front, creating a shield in front of your and body face.
4. You can slightly rotate your body towards your back side as the assault comes towards you, further deflecting the attack.

During all Defenses:
- Use loud defensive verbalizations (NO, STOP, GET BACK, STOP RESISTING, etc.) to direct the aggressor to stop attacking you.
- Use defensive movements (Escape!)

After all Defenses:
- Follow agency policies and procedures in regard to self-defense.
- Report and Document immediately.

High Block Defense

High Block Defense
Is a technique that teaches individuals how to deflect an imminent assault to your head.

Objective
Demonstrate how to properly use a defensive high block against a physical assault to your head.

Performance—High Block Defense
1. Assume the bladed stance.
2. Bring your chin down.
3. Bring your arm up in front of your face with your palm out.
4. Your hands can be open or closed.
5. You can use your support arm, strong arm or both arms to defend against an attack to your head.

During all Defenses:
- Use loud defensive verbalizations (NO, STOP, GET BACK, STOP RESISTING, etc.) to direct the aggressor to stop attacking you.

- Use defensive movements (Escape!)

After all Defenses:
- Follow agency policies and procedures in regard to self-defense.
- Report and Document immediately.

Middle Block Defense

Middle Block Defense
Is a technique that teaches individuals how to deflect an imminent rushing assault or grappling attack towards you.

Objective
Demonstrate how to properly use a defensive middle block against a physical assault coming at you.

Performance—Middle Block Defense
1. Assume the bladed stance.
2. Bring both arms up in front of you (palms out).
3. Push the aggressor away at the shoulders or torso area.
4. Use side-to-side movement after the middle block defense to get into a position of advantage or to continue to defend.

During all Defenses:
- Use loud repetitive defensive verbalizations (NO, STOP, GET BACK, STOP RESISTING, etc.) to direct the aggressor to stop attacking you.
- Use defensive movements (Escape!)

After all Defenses:
- Follow agency policies and procedures in regard to self-defense.
- Report and Document immediately.

Outside Block Defense

Outside Block Defense

Is a technique that teaches individuals how to deflect an imminent assault to either side of your body.

Objective

Demonstrate how to properly use a defensive outside block against a physical assault coming to either side of your body.

Performance—Outside Block Defense

1. Assume the bladed stance.
2. Bring either your right or left (or both) up arms in front of your body and pivot towards the direction of the attack.
3. Your hands can be open or closed.
4. You can use your support arm, strong arm or both arms to defend against an attack to either side of your body.

During all Defenses:

- Use loud defensive verbalizations (NO, STOP, GET BACK, STOP RESISTING, etc.) to direct the aggressor to stop attacking you.
- Use defensive movements (Escape!)

After all Defenses:

- Follow agency policies and procedures in regard to self-defense.
- Report and Document immediately.

Low Block Defense

Low Block Defense
Is a technique that teaches individuals how to deflect an imminent attack to lower area of the body.

Objective
Demonstrate how to properly use a defensive low block against a physical assault coming to the lower part of your body.

Performance—Low Block Defense
1. Assume the bladed stance.
2. Bring either your right or left (or both) arm down, sweeping in front of your body and moving the attack away.
3. Your hands can be open or closed.
4. You can use your support arm, strong arm or both arms to defend against an attack to the lower area of your body.

During all Defenses:
- Use loud defensive verbalizations (NO, STOP, GET BACK, STOP RESISTING, etc.) to direct the aggressor to stop attacking you.
- Use defensive movements (Escape!)

After all Defenses:
- Follow agency policies and procedures in regard to self-defense.
- Report and Document immediately.

Module Eight – Personal Defense Skills & Techniques (Optional)

Palm Heel Defense

Palm Heel Defense
The palm heel defense counter strike may be a reasonable defense from an attack of an aggressor.

Objective
Demonstrate how to correctly use a palm heel defense technique to defend against an attack from an aggressor.

Performance—Palm Heel Defense
1. Assume the bladed stance.
2. Position your strong or support hand with your heel extended outward.
3. Fingers are in a claw position and have nothing to do with the defense.
4. You can pivot your body forward thrusting your heel into the desired area of impact.

During all Defenses:
- Use loud defensive verbalizations (NO, STOP, GET BACK, STOP RESISTING, etc.) to direct the aggressor to stop attacking you.
- Use defensive movements (Escape!)

After all Defenses:
- Follow agency policies and procedures in regard to self-defense.
- Report and Document immediately.

Fist Defense

Fist Defense
The fist defense counter strike may be a reasonable defense from an attack of an aggressor.

Objective
Demonstrate how to correctly use a fist defense technique to defend against an attack from an aggressor.

Performance—Fist Defense
1. Assume the bladed stance.
2. Position your strong or support hand with your fingers clenched tightly into your palm.
3. Vertical or horizontal fist positions can be used.
4. You can pivot your body forward thrusting your fist into the desired area of impact.

Caution: Proper fist position is required to avoid injuring yourself.

During all Defenses:
- Use loud defensive verbalizations (NO, STOP, GET BACK, STOP RESISTING, etc.) to direct the aggressor to stop attacking you.
- Use defensive movements (Escape!)

After all Defenses:
- Follow agency policies and procedures in regard to self-defense.
- Report and Document immediately.

Hammer Fist Defense

Hammer Fist Defense

The hammer fist defense counter strike may be a reasonable defense from an attack of an aggressor.

Objective

Demonstrate how to correctly use a fist defense technique to defend against an attack from an aggressor.

Performance—Hammer Fist Defense

1. Assume the bladed stance.
2. Position your strong or support hand with your fingers clenched tightly into your palm.
3. Vertical, diagonal or horizontal hammer fist defenses may be used.
4. You can pivot your body forward thrusting your fist into the desired area of impact.

Caution: Proper fist position is required to avoid injuring yourself.

During all Defenses:

- Use loud defensive verbalizations (NO, STOP, GET BACK, STOP RESISTING, etc.) to direct the aggressor to stop attacking you.
- Use defensive movements (Escape!)

After all Defenses:

- Follow agency policies and procedures in regard to self-defense.
- Report and Document immediately.

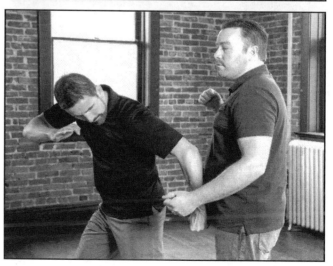

Forearm Defense

Forearm Defense

The forearm defense counter strike may be a reasonable defense from an attack of an aggressor.

Objective

Demonstrate how to correctly use a forearm defense technique to defend against an attack from an aggressor.

Performance—Forearm Defense

1. Assume the bladed stance.
2. Position your strong or support hand with your fingers clenched tightly or in an open position.
3. Vertical, diagonal or horizontal forearm defenses may be used.
4. You can pivot your body forward or backward thrusting your forearm into the desired area of impact.

During all Defenses:

- Use loud defensive verbalizations (NO, STOP, GET BACK, STOP RESISTING, etc.) to direct the aggressor to stop attacking you.
- Use defensive movements (Escape!)

After all Defenses:

- Follow agency policies and procedures in regard to self-defense.
- Report and Document immediately.

Elbow Defense

Elbow Defense

The elbow defense counter strike may be a reasonable defense from an attack of an aggressor.

Objective

Demonstrate how to correctly use an elbow defense technique to defend against an attack from an aggressor.

Performance—Elbow Defense

1. Assume the bladed stance.
2. When using your strong/support hand elbow, you can blade your hand or clenched hand tightly.
3. Vertical, frontal and rear elbow defenses may be used.
4. You can pivot your body forward or backward thrusting your elbow into the desired area of impact.

During all Defenses:

- Use loud defensive verbalizations (NO, STOP, GET BACK, STOP RESISTING, etc.) to direct the aggressor to stop attacking you.
- Use defensive movements (Escape!)

After all Defenses:

- Follow agency policies and procedures in regard to self-defense.
- Report and Document immediately.

Knee Defense

Knee Defense
The knee defense counter strike may be a reasonable defense from an attack of an aggressor.

Objective
Demonstrate how to correctly use a knee defense technique to defend against an attack from an aggressor.

Performance—Knee Defense
1. Assume the bladed stance.
2. Your support or strong knee can be used.
3. Your foot should be pulled back when defending, creating a pointed knee for impact.
4. You can pivot your body forward thrusting your knee into the desired area of impact.

During all Defenses:
- Use loud defensive verbalizations (NO, STOP, GET BACK, STOP RESISTING, etc.) to direct the aggressor to stop attacking you.
- Use defensive movements (Escape!)

After all Defenses:
- Follow agency policies and procedures in regard to self-defense.
- Report and Document immediately.

Kick Defense

Kick Defense

The kick defense counter strike may be a reasonable defense from an attack of an aggressor.

Objective

Demonstrate how to correctly use a frontal and side kick defense technique to defend against an attack from an aggressor.

Performance—Frontal and Side Kick Defense

1. Assume the bladed stance.
2. Your support or strong side can be used for frontal and sidekicks.
3. For the frontal kick, your toes should be pulled back.
4. For the side kick use the edge of your outer foot.

Caution: Balance may be compromised when deploying a defensive kick.

During all Defenses:

- Use loud defensive verbalizations (NO, STOP, GET BACK, STOP RESISTING, etc.) to direct the aggressor to stop attacking you.
- Use defensive movements (Escape!)

After all Defenses:

- Follow agency policies and procedures in regard to self-defense.
- Report and Document immediately.

Module Nine – Weapon Retention Techniques

Holstered Weapon Retention

Holstered weapon retention is the understanding of your personal equipment and the defensive skills that may be used to keep your weapon holstered.

Objective
Demonstrate how to correctly retain your weapon in its holster while using personal defensive skills and movements.

Performance
Holstered Weapon Retention
1. Assume the bladed stance.
2. Familiarize yourself with your personal holster and its function.
3. Practice personal defensive skills and movements while retaining personal weapon.

Weapon retention may be used for any personal defensive weapon an officer carries (firearm, chemical sprays, baton, Taser®, etc.)

During all Defenses:
- Use loud defensive verbalizations
  (NO, STOP, GET BACK, STOP RESISTING, etc.) to direct the aggressor to stop attacking you.
- Use defensive movements (Escape if needed)

After all Defenses:
- Follow agency policies and procedures in regard to arrest and control.
- Report and Document immediately.

Elbow, Single Hand and Two Hand Weapon Retention

The officer's elbows and hands may be used to assist the officer in retaining his/her personal weapon.

Objective
Demonstrate how to effectively retain your personal weapon using your elbows and hands.

Performance
Holstered Weapon Retention
1. Assume the bladed stance.
2. Position your elbow, single hand (usually strong) or both hands over your personal defensive weapon.
3. Personal defensive skills and movements may be used for retaining personal weapon.

During all Defenses:
- Use loud defensive verbalizations (NO, STOP, GET BACK, STOP RESISTING, etc.) to direct the aggressor to stop attacking you.
- Use defensive movements (Escape if needed)

After all Defenses:
- Follow agency policies and procedures in regard to arrest and control.
- Report and Document immediately.

Module Ten – Post Incident Response & Documentation

It's vital for all employers to have a **Post-Incident Response** protocol. The following points are guideline for the proper and most efficient response to a violent incident.

Triage (Medical/Hazmat): Triage is the process of determining the priority of patients/victims treatments based on the severity of their condition. Initial first-aid treatment and protocols for hazardous materials/clean-up should be handled immediately.

Report to the Police, Security, Risk Management, Human Resources etc. Follow standard operating procedures in regard to reporting incidents.

Consider All Involved—staff, guests, visitors, patients or anyone who was witness to the incident should be treated accordingly for medical and stress debriefing.

Provide for Incident Debriefing: Debriefing allows those involved with the incident to process the event and reflect on its impact. Depending on the situation, a thorough debriefing may need to take place. Even those not specifically involved in an incident may suffer emotional and psychological trauma.

Critical Incident Stress Debriefing (CISD) is a specific technique designed to assist others in dealing with physical or psychological symptoms that are generally associated with critical incident trauma exposure. Research on the effectiveness of critical incident debriefing techniques has demonstrated that individuals who are provided critical stress debriefing within a 24- to 72-hour window after the critical incident and experience have less short-term and long-term crisis reactions and psychological trauma.

Employee Assistance Programs (EAP) EAPs are intended to help employees deal with work/personal problems that might adversely impact their work performance, health, and well-being. EAPs generally include assessment, short-term counseling and referral services for employees and their household members. Employee benefit programs offered by many employers, typically in conjunction with a health insurance plans, provide for payment for EAPs.

Document incident to include any follow-up investigations: Post incident documentation is absolutely critical for reducing liability risk, preventing reoccurrences and follow-up investigations.

Initiate corrective actions to prevent reoccurrences: Preventing similar future incidents, involves taking proactive corrective actions. Agency management, supervision, security, risk management, employee safety committees, environment of care committees, etc. should initiate, track and follow up on corrective actions

Post Incident Documentation

- **Who-What-Where-When-Why-How**
The first rule in post incident documentation is the "who, what, where, when, why and how" rule of reporting. After writing an incident narrative, double-check to see if you have included the first rule of reporting.

- **Witnesses (who was there?):** Make sure to include anyone who was a witness to the incident. Staff, visitors, guests and support services (police, fire, EMS, etc.) can be valuable witnesses should an incident be litigated.

- **Narrative Characteristics:** A proper narrative should describe in detail the characteristics of the aggressor. The aggressor's actions are very important to note, because using force and self-defense are based on the amount of resistance encountered.
  - How did the subject respond to your verbal commands?
  - What kind of verbal and non-verbal language did the aggressor communicate?
  - How did the aggressor respond to your force/self-defense?

- **Before, During and After:** A thorough incident report will describe what happened before, during and after the incident. Details matter!
  - How did you approach?
  - Officers should identify themselves to establish authority.
  - Describe what you observed and what your verbal commands were.

- **1st Person vs. 3rd Person:** The account of an incident can be described in first person or third person. This can be specific to your agency protocols or the preference of the person documenting the incident.

- **Post Follow-Up (track and trend):** Most agencies use electronic documentation, which allows for easy retrieval, tracking and trending. Using technology assists agencies to follow up and initiate proactive corrections.

- **Follow Standard Operating Procedures:** Whether it is handwriting incident reports or electronic documentation and charting, staff should consistently and thoroughly document all incidents relating to violence in the workplace.

Elements of Reporting Force

Elements of Reporting Self-Defense or Force

Report and Document: After any situation involving defense of yourself or another person, proper documentation and reporting is crucial. The events of the assault or attempted assault should be reported to security/police. The police/security will document the incident and start an investigation. You should also document the account for your own internal records. This can protect you in a possible legal situation that could arise out of using force to defend yourself. As you document your account of the incident make sure to report to security/police any details you missed during your initial report to them.

What type of force/self-defense was used during the incident? Be specific in your documentation regarding the type of control, defense and force that was used during the incident.

How long did the incident and resistance last? Important to note the length of the resistance, as this is a factor relative to exhaustion and increasing the level of force.

Was any de-escalation used?
Verbal and non-verbal de-escalation techniques should be noted.

Were you in fear of injury (bodily harm) to yourself, others or the subject? Fear is a distressing emotion aroused by perceived threat, impending danger, evil or pain.

If so, Why? Fear is a basic survival mechanism occurring in response to a specific stimulus, such as pain or the threat of danger.

Thoroughly explain, and make sure to document completely. The importance of documentation cannot be over emphasized. Documentation ensures proper training standards are met, policies and procedures are understood, certification standards are met, liability and risk management mitigation, and departmental and organizational requirements are maintained. A ruling in the United States, Whiteley v. Warden, 410 U.S. 560 (1971), states, that if it is not documented (training and the incident specifics), it did not happen. Therefore, if you do not document your training, a court may rule that training did not occur.

Special Note: Every person must take into consideration their moral, legal and ethical beliefs, rights and understandings when using any type of force to defend themselves or others. **Personal Safety Training Inc.** makes no legal declaration, representation or claim as to what force should be used or not used during a self-defense/assault incident or situation. Each trainee must take into consideration their ability, agency policies and procedures and state and federal laws.

Module Eleven – Healthcare Restraint Holds/Applications

Policies and Procedures for Restraining Patients

The Healthcare Defensive Tactics System™ involves specific techniques and interventions for controlling and restraining a subject in the healthcare environment. These techniques are complimentary to the defensive tactics interventions in the first ten modules. The difference is that healthcare security professionals are involved in specific healthcare restraint applications prompted by licensed medical professionals directing them to restrain a patient in a face up (supine) position.

This section of the training begins with teaching individuals how to stand a subject who has been taken down into a prone position without the application of handcuffs. From this position a subject can be escorted to a healthcare bed where they can be placed and healthcare restraints can be applied.

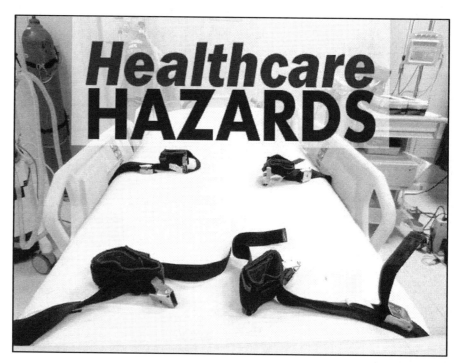

Personal Safety Training Inc. does not dictate policies or procedures for the use of any arrest, detention, control and restraint, self-defense, use of force or any physical intervention authorized for use by a department/agency or private individual. The suggestions, options and techniques disseminated during this training program are simply that, suggestions, options and techniques. Each individual, department or agency is responsible for developing their own "policies and procedures" regarding use of force, self-defense, physical intervention or physical restraints/control, arrest/detention for their personnel.

This course stresses the importance of knowing your agency policies and procedures in regard to using force and defending yourself or another person. The Healthcare Defensive Tactics System™ training is intended to give the trainee the basic understanding of self-defense, use of force, control and restraint, reasonable force and basic legal definitions of force.

Standing the Prone Subject

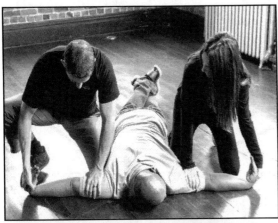

Standing the Prone Subject
Is a technique that teaches an individual(s) how to stand a prone controlled subject.

Objective
Demonstrate how to stand a subject who has been placed in a prone controlled position (one or two individuals are needed).

Performance—Standing the Prone Subject
1. Once control is established verbalize to the subject to place their hands in the push up position.

2. Direct them to push their knees up under them to prepare to stand.

3. Maintain contact with the subject arms and wrists and also prepare to stand up as well.

4. Bring one of the subject's wrists to the holster position on the side of your body.

5. Once control is established by holstering one wrist, the second person will holster the subjects other wrist.

6. Once both wrists are holstered have the subject raise one knee.

7. You will need to have subject raise their torso in order to get them to place one knee if front of them.

8. Ask subject to then stand up completely. Direct the subject where you want them to go.

Caution: Verbalization and constant control is the key to standing a prone controlled subject.
Maintain your balance and be prepared to escape if needed.

Healthcare Hazards

Healthcare Restraint Holds/Applications

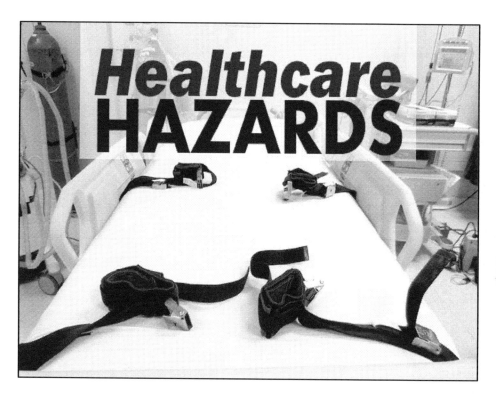

- Using restraints to control violence is acceptable in certain cases, but clinical policy and procedures must be rigidly adhered to.

- Restraint use is very controversial and not always understood by staff. Acceptability of restraint use should be carefully identified and approved by medical staff.

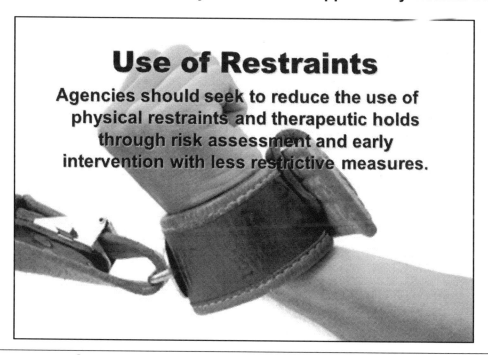

Supine Healthcare Restraint

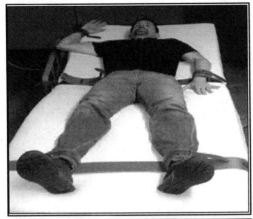

Supine Healthcare Restraint

The following pictures depict a 4pt healthcare restraint for a behavioral/violent person restraint application.

Objective

Demonstrate how to hold and apply healthcare restraints to a combative/violent individual.

Performance—Supine Restraint Hold/Application

1. Once staff (2 persons) have placed an individual on the bed they (+ 2 other staff) will hold them down on either side of the elbow and knee. Not on joint!
2. A 5th staff person can then apply restraints to the ankles and wrists.
3. By keeping one arm raised above head, it reduces the individual's ability to use their core strength and resist.
4. A 6th person may be needed to control the individual's head.
5. A 7th staff person may be needed to control the individual's feet until restraints can be applied.

Note: Restraints can be removed for a 3pt, 2pt or even 1pt restraint. Follow your SOP's.

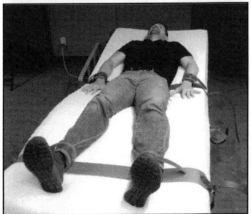

During all Defenses:

- Use loud repetitive defensive verbalizations (NO, STOP, STOP RESISTING, etc.) to direct the aggressor to stop resisting you.

Always:

- Follow agency policies and procedures in regard to restraint and seclusion.
- Report and Document immediately.

Risk Factors for Restraints

Risk Factors for Restraints:

- ➢ Patients who smoke

- ➢ Positional Asphyxiation

- ➢ Patients with deformities

- ➢ Improper restraining Techniques

- ➢ Incomplete medical assessment

- ➢ Improper restraints, room and beds

- ➢ Insufficient staff orientation and training

- ➢ Supine position may predispose them to aspiration

- ➢ Prone may predispose them to suffocation

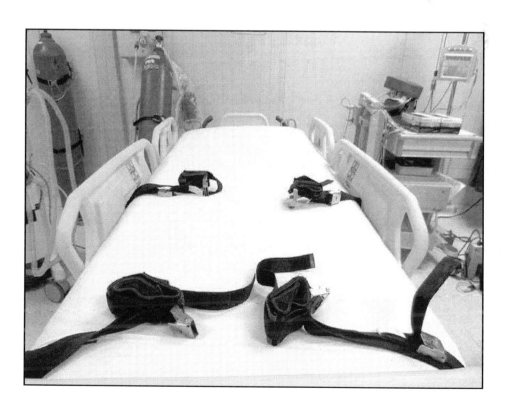

Strategies for Reducing Risk

➢ Reduce use of physical restraints and holds through risk assessments and early interventions.

➢ Clarification of restraint use in clinical protocols.

➢ See alternatives to restraint use (de-escalation techniques).

➢ Enhance staff orientation/education regarding alternatives and proper application.

➢ Develop structured procedures / competency for consistent application of restraints.

➢ Develop safety guidelines and continuous observation of those restrained.

➢ The "one-hour" rule.

➢ Utilize patient quiet rooms/seclusion rooms.

➢ Revise the staffing model.

➢ Increase awareness of medical/surgical vs. behavioral restraints.

➢ Comply to JCAHO and State/Federal Standards

Strategies for Reducing Risk

➤ If patient is restrained in the supine position, ensure that head is free to rotate and when possible, the head of the bed is elevated to minimize the risk of aspiration.

➤ If patient must be controlled in the prone position, ensure that airway is unobstructed at all times (do not cover or bury the patients face). Ensure that patient can expand their lungs to properly breathe (do not put any pressure on their back).

  • Special caution is required for children, elderly patients and very obese patients.

➤ Never place a towel, bag or other cover over a patients face.

➤ Do not restrain a patient in a bed with unprotected split side rails.

➤ Do not use certain types of restraints, such as high vests and waist restraints.

➤ Ensure patient is properly searched and free of weapons and smoking materials.

  • This would also include limiting access from friends and family

Policy and Procedures should be adhered to for all Healthcare Restraint Applications/Holds.

Chemical Restraints

A **chemical restraint** is a form of medical restraint in which a drug is used to restrict the freedom or movement of a patient, or in some cases, to sedate a patient. These are used in emergency, acute, and psychiatric settings to control aggressive patients who are interfering with their care or who are otherwise harmful to themselves or others.

Drugs that are often used as chemical restraints include benzodiazepines (such as Lorazepam (Ativan), Midazolam (Versed), or Diazepam (Valium). Haloperidol (Haldol) is a drug chemically unrelated to benzodiazepines and is also popular for chemical restraint, without the potentially dangerous side effects of benzodiazepine drugs.

Any use of chemical restraints must be authorized and administered by a licensed clinician or doctor.

Positional Asphyxia

Positional asphyxia is a form of asphyxia which occurs when someone's position prevents them from breathing adequately. A small but significant number of people die suddenly and without apparent reason during restraint by police, prison (corrections) officers and health care staff. Positional asphyxia may be a factor in some of these deaths.

- Positional asphyxia is a potential danger of some physical restraint techniques.
- People may die from positional asphyxia by simply getting themselves into a breathing-restricted position they cannot get out of, either through carelessness or as a consequence of another accident.

Research has suggested that restraining a person in a face down position is likely to cause greater restriction of breathing than restraining a person face up. Many law enforcement and health personnel are now taught to avoid restraining people face down or to do so only for a very short period of time.

Risk factors which may increase the chance of death include: Obesity, Prior Cardiac or Respiratory Problems, Alcohol Intoxication, Illicit drugs such as cocaine and Excited Delirium "Bizarre or Frenzied Behavior" (mental disease including psychosis and schizophrenia and/or drug intoxication).

Excited Delirium

Excited delirium is a controversial term used to explain deaths of individuals in police custody, in which the person being arrested or restrained shows some combination of agitation, violent or bizarre behavior, insensitivity to pain, elevated body temperature, or increased strength. It has been listed as a cause of death by some medical examiners.

- The term has no formal medical recognition and is not recognized in the *Diagnostic and Statistical Manual of Mental Disorders.* There may also be a controversial link between "excited delirium" deaths and the use of Tasers to subdue agitated people.

- Almost all subjects who have died during restraint have engaged in extreme levels of physical resistance against the restraint for a prolonged period of time.

- Other issues in the way the subject is restrained can also increase the risk of death; for example, kneeling or otherwise placing weight on the subject and particularly any type of restraint hold around the subject's neck.

Static Air Drills

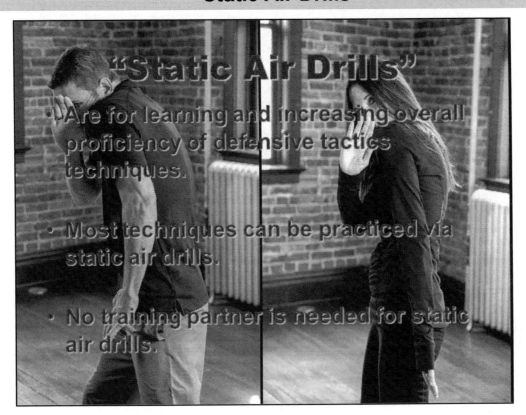

Blocking Drills

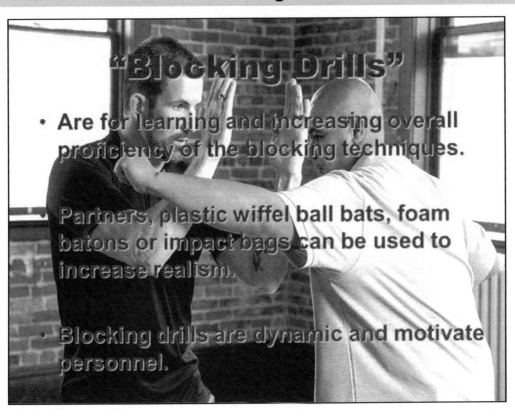

Impact Drills

Partner Drills

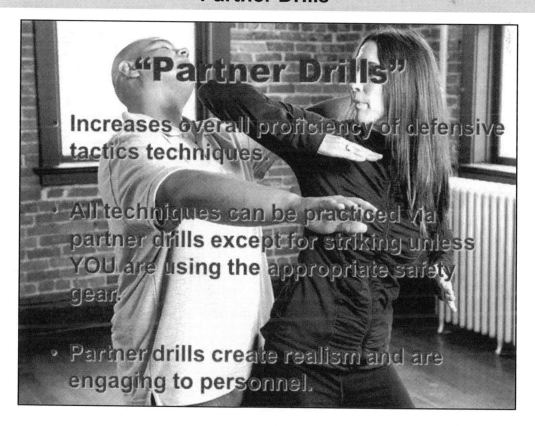

Positioning Drills

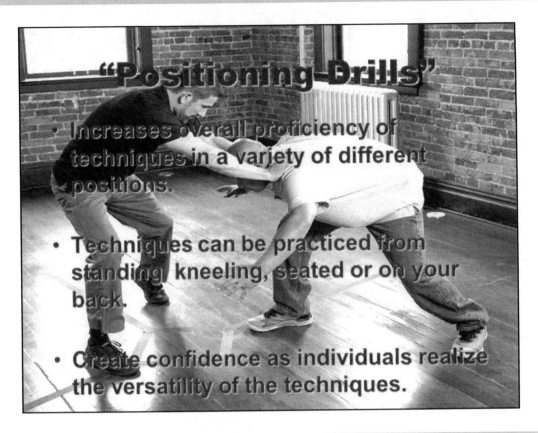

"Positioning Drills"

• Increases overall proficiency of techniques in a variety of different positions.

• Techniques can be practiced from standing, kneeling, seated or on your back.

• Create confidence as individuals realize the versatility of the techniques.

Combination Drills

"Combination Drills"

• Increases overall proficiency of techniques with combinations of blocking, defending & control techniques.

• Combination drills can be practiced using defenses, blocks, movements, bags and partners.

• YOU are only limited by your imagination.

Healthcare Defensive Tactics System™ Review

✓ **Use of Force**

✓ **Defensive Tactics Fundamentals**

✓ **Contact and Cover Positioning**

✓ **Escort Strategies and Techniques**

✓ **Control & Decentralization Techniques**

✓ **Handcuffing Techniques**

✓ **Defensive Blocking Techniques**

✓ **Personal Defensive Skills & Techniques**

✓ **Weapon Retention Techniques**

✓ **Post Incident Response and Documentation**

✓ **Healthcare Restraint Holds/Applications**

Bibliography, Reference Guide and Recommended Reading

Books, CD's, DVD's and Websites

Adams, Terry and Rob. *Seminar Production Business: Your Step by Step Guide to Success.* Entrepreneur Press, Canada 2003.

Albrect, Steve. *Surviving Street Patrol: The Officer's Guide to Safe and Effective Policing.* Paladin Press, Boulder, CO 2001.

Amdur, Ellis. *Dueling with O-sensei: Grappling with the Myth of the Warrior Sage.* Edgework, Seattle, WA 2000.

Andersen, Peter A. *The Complete Idiot's Guide to Body Language.* Alpha Books, Indianapolis, IN 2004.

Andrews, Andy. *The Travelers Gift: Seven Decisions that Determine Personal Success.* Nelsen Books, Nashville Tennessee, 2002.

Arapakis, Maria. *Soft Power: How to Speak Up, Set Limits, and Say No Without Losing Your Lover, Your Job, or Your Friends.* Warner Books Inc. NY, NY 1990.

Artwhohl, Alexis & Christensen, Loren. *Deadly Force Encounters: What Cops need to know to mentally and physically prepare for and survive a gunfight.* Paladin Press, Boulder, CO 1997.

ASIS International. *Security Management Magazine.* www.securitymanagment.com 2006-2016.

Brown, Tom. *Survival Guides: Americas Bestselling Wilderness Series.* Berkley Books, New York, 1984.

Byrnes, John D. *Before Conflict: Preventing Aggressive Behavior.* Scarecrow Press, Lanham, Maryland and Oxford 2002.

Canfield, Jack and Switzer, Janet. *The Success Principles: How to Get from Where You Are to Where You Want to Be.* Harper Collins Publishers, NY, NY 2005.

Canfield, Jack and Bunch, Jim. *The Ultimate Life Workshop: 7 Strategies for Creating the Ultimate Life.* Live Workshop - February 2008.

Carnegie, Dale. *Golden Book.* www.dalecarnegie.com

Carnegie, Dale. *How to Win Friends & Influence People*. Pocket Books, NY, NY 1936.

Chodron, Thubten. *Working With Anger*. Snow Lion Publication, Ithaca, NY 2001.

Christenson, Loren. *DEFENSIVE TACTICS: Modern Arrest & Control Techniques for Today's Police Warrior*. Turtle Press, Washington, DC 2008.

Christenson, Loren. *Fighting in the Clinch: Vicious Strikes, Street Wrestling, and Gouges for Real Fights*. Paladin Press, Boulder, CO 2009.

Christensen, Loren. *The Way Alone: Your Path to Excellence in the Martial Arts*. Paladin Press, Boulder, CO 1987.

Christensen, Loren. *Warriors: On Living with Courage, Discipline and Honor*. Paladin Press, Boulder, CO 2004.

Covey, Stephen R. *The 7 Habits of Highly Effective People: Powerful Lessons in Personal Change*. Fireside, NY, NY 1989.

Covey, Stephen R. *The 8th Habit: From Effectiveness to Greatness*. Better Life Media, DVD and CD, 2004.

Day Laura, *Practical Intuition*. Villard Books, NY, NY 1996.

DeBecker, Gavin. *The Gift of Fear*. Dell Publishing, NY, NY 1997.

DeBecker, Gavin. *Fear Less: Real Truth about Risk, Safety, and Security in a Time of Terrorism*. Little Brown and Company, Boston, NY, London 2002.

DeBecker, Gavin & Taylor, Tom & Marquart, Jeff. *Just 2 Seconds: Using Time and Space to Defeat Assassins*. The Gavin DeBecker Center for the Study and Reduction of Violence a not-for-profit foundation, Studio City, CA 2008.

DeBecker, Gavin. *Protecting the Gift: Keeping Children and Teenagers Safe (and Parents Sane)*. A Dell Trade Paperback, NY, NY 1999.

Deshimaru, Taisen. *The Zen Way to the Martial Arts: A Japanese Master Reveals the Secrets of the Samurai*. Penguin Compass. NY, NY 1982.

DeMasco, Steve. *The Shaolin Way: 10 Modern Secrets of Survival from a Shaolin Kung Fu Grandmaster*. Harper, NY, NY 2006.

Divine, Mark. *The WAY of the SEAL: Think Like an Elite Warrior to Lead and Succeed.* Readers Digest, White Plains, NY 2013.

Dyer, Wayne. *The Power of Intention; Learning to Co-Create your world your way.* Hay House, CA 2004.

Eckman, Paul. *Emotions Revealed: Recognizing Faces and Feelings to Improve Communication and Emotional Life.* Henry Holt & Company, NY, NY 2007.

Eckman, Paul. *Telling Lies.* WW. Norton Company, NY and London. 1991.

Eggerichs, Emerson. *Love & Respect: The Love She Most Desires and The respect he Desperately Needs.* Gale Cengage Learning. US 2010.

Fowler, David. *Be Safe Not Sorry, the Art and Science of keeping YOU and your family Safe from Crime and Violence.* Personal Safety Training Inc. Coeur d Alene, ID 2011.

Fowler, David. *Violence In The Workplace: Education, Prevention & Mitigation.* Personal Safety Training Inc. Coeur d Alene, ID 2012.

Fowler, David. *To Serve and Protect: Providing SERVICE while maintaining SAFETY in the Workplace.* Personal Safety Training Inc. Coeur d Alene, ID 2015.

Fowler, David. *Violence In The Workplace II: Education, Prevention & Mitigation Strategies and Techniques.* Personal Safety Training Inc. Coeur d Alene, ID 2016.

Funakoshi, Gichen. *Karate-Do My Way of Life.* Kodansha International, Tokyo, NY. London, 1975.

Gallo, Carmine. *Inspire Your Audience: 7 Keys to Influential Presentations.* Paper. Communication Skills Coach – Author of Fire Them Up!

Gardner, Daniel. *The Science of Fear: How the Culture of Fear MANIPULATES YOUR BRAIN.* Penguin Books Ltd, Strand, London 2009

Garner, Bryan. *Black's Law Dictionary: Seventh Edition.* West Group, St. Paul, MN, 1999.

Gawain, Shakti. *Creative Visualization.* New World Library, Novato, CA 2002.

Gawain, Shakti. *Developing Intuition: Practical Guide for Daily Life.* New World Library, Novato, CA 2000.

Gilligan, James. *VIOLENCE: Reflections on a National Epidemic.* Vintage Books, NY 1996.

Gladwell, Malcolm. *Blink*. Little, Brown & Company, NY 2005.

Glennon, Jim. *Arresting Communication: Essential Interaction Skills for Law Enforcement*. LifeLine Training & Caliber Press, Elmhurst, IL 2010.

Goleman, Daniel. *Emotional Intelligence*. Bantom Books, NY, NY 2005.

Gray, John. *Beyond Mars and Venus*. Better Life Media, DVD and CD, 2004.

Gregory, Hamilton. *Public Speaking for College and Career: Fifth Edition*. McGraw-Hill, Boston 1999.

Gross, Linden. *Surviving A Stalker: Everything you need to know to keep yourself safe*. Marlowe and Company, NY, NY 2000.

Grossman, Dave & Christensen, Loren. *On Combat: The Psychology of Deadly Conflict in War and Peace*. PPCT Research, IL 2004.

Grossman, Dave & DeGaetano, Gloria. *Stop Teaching our Kids to Kill: A call to action against TV, Movie & Video Game Violence*. Crown Publishers, NY, NY 1999.

Harrell, Keith. *Attitude is Everything: 10 Life Changing Steps to Turning Attitude Into Action*. Harper Collins Publishing, NY, NY 1999.

Hawkins, David R, MD. *Power vs. Force: The Hidden Determinants of Human Behavior*. Veritas, Sedona, AZ 2004.

Headley, Steve. *Assault Prevention Workshop*. Assault Prevention Workshops, LLC 2009.

Hyams, Joe. *Zen in the Martial Arts*. Bantam Books, Toronto, NY, London, Sydney, Auckland, 1982.

IAHSS. *Basic Training Manual and Study Guide for Healthcare Security Officers*. Lombard, IL 1995.

IAHSS. *Journal of Healthcare Protection Management*. Bayside, NY 2008-2016.

Jo-Ellan Dimitrius, Ph.D., and Mark Mazzarella. *Reading People: How to Understand people and Predict their Behavior-Anytime, Anyplace*. Ballantine Books, NY, NY 1999.

Kane, Lawrence A. *Surviving Armed Assaults*. YMAA Publication Center, Boston MA 2006.

Kinnaird, Brian. *Use of Force: Expert Guidance for Decisive Force Response*. Looseleaf Law Publications, Flushing, NY 2003.

Krebs & Henry & Gabriele. *When Violence Erupts: A Survival Guide for Emergency Responders*. The C.V. Mosby Company, St. Louis, Baltimore, Philadelphia, Toronto, 1990.

Larkin, Tim and Ranck-Buhr, Chris. *How to Survive The Most Critical 5 Seconds of Your Life*. The TFT Group. Sequim, WA 2008.

Lawler, Jennifer. *Dojo Wisdom: 100 Simple Ways to Become a Stronger, Calmer, more Courageous Person*. Penguin Compass, NY, NY 2003.

Leaf, Caroline. *Switch on your Brain: The key to Peak Happiness, Thinking, and Health*. Baker Books, Grand Rapids, MI 2013.

Lee, Bruce. *Tao of Jeet Kune Do*. Ohara Publications, Santa Clarita, CA 1975.

Lee, Johnny. *Addressing Domestic Violence in the Workplace*. HRD Press, Inc. Amherst, MA 2005.

Lee, Linda. *The Bruce Lee Story*. Ohara Publications, Santa Clarita, CA 1989.

Lion, John, MD. *Evaluation and Management of the Violent Patient: Guidelines in the Hospital and Institution*. Charles C. Thomas Publisher, Springfield, IL 1972.

Little, John. *The Warrior Within: The philosophies of Bruce Lee to better understand the world around you and achieve a rewarding life*. Contemporary Books, Chicago, IL 1996.

Loehr, James and Migdwo, Jeffrey. Breathe In Breathe Out: Inhale Energy and Exhale Stress By Guiding and Controlling Your Breathing. Time Life Books, Alexandria, VI 1986.

Lorenz, Conrad. *On Aggression*. MJF Book. NY 1963.

Machowicz, Richard J. *Unleash The Warrior Within: Develop the Focus, Discipline, Confidence and Courage You Need to Achieve Unlimited Goals*. Marlowe & Company, NY 2002.

Mackay, Harvey. "Harvey Mackay's Column This Week." Weekly e-mail publication, www.harveymackay.com.

MacYoung, Marc "Animal." *Ending Violence Quickly: How Bouncers, Bodyguards and Other Security Professionals Handle Ugly Situations.* Paladin Press, Boulder, CO 1993.

Maggio, Rosalie. *How to Say It: Choice Words, Phrases, Sentences, and Paragraphs for Every Situation.* Prentice Hall Press, NY, NY 2001.

Maltz, Maxwell MD. *Psycho-Cybernetics: A New Way to Get More Living Out Of Life.* Essandress, NY, NY 1960.

Marcinko, Richard. *The Rogue Warriors Strategy For Success.* Pocket Books, NY, NY 1997.

Mason, Tom & Chandley Mark. *Managing Violence and Aggression: A Manual for Nurses and Health Care Workers.* Churchill Livingstone, Edinburgh, 1999.

McGrew, James. *Think Safe: Practical Measures to Increase Security at Home, at Work, and Throughout Life.* Cameo Publications, Hilton Head Island, SC, 2004

McTaggart, Lynne. *The Intention Experiment: Using Your thoughts to Change Your Life and the World.* Free Press, NY, NY 2007.

Medina, John. *Brain Rules: 12 Principles for Surviving and Thriving at Work, Home, and School.* Pear Press, Seattle, WA 2008.

Miller, Rory. *FACING VIOLENCE: Preparing for the Unexpected-Ethically, Emotionally, Physically, Without Going to Prison.* YMAA Publication Center, Wolfeboro, NH 2011.

MOAB Training International, Inc. MOAB® Instructor Manual. 2009.

Monadnock Police Training Council. MEB Instructor Manual. 2003.

Monadnock Police Training Council. PR-24® Instructor Manual. 2003.

Monadnock Police Training Council. MDTS Instructor Manual. 2003.

Murphy, Joseph, Dr. *The Power of Your Subconscious Mind.* Bantam Books, NY, Toronto, London, Sidney, Auckland 2000.

Musashi, Miyamoto. Translated by Thomas Cleary. *The Book of Five Rings.* Shambala, Boston and London 2003.

Norris, Chuck. *The Secret Power Within: Zen Solutions to Real Problems.* Broadway Books, NY 1996.

Norris, Chuck. *Winning Tournament Karate.* Ohara Publications, Burbank, CA 1975.

Nowicki, Ed. *Total Survival.* Performance Dimensions, Powers Lake, MI 1993.

Omartian, Stormie. *PRAYER WARRIOR: The Power of Praying Your Way to Victory*. Harvest House Publishers, Eugene, OR 2013.

Ouellette, Roland W. *Management of Aggressive Behavior*. Performance Dimension Publishing, Powers Lake, WI 1993.

Palumbo, Dennis. *The Secrets of Hakkoryu Jujutsu: Shodan Tactics*. Paladin Press Boulder, CO 1987.

Parker, S.L. *212 the extra degree*. The Walk the Talk Co. 2005 www.walkthetalk.com.

Patire, Tom. *Tom Patire's Personal Protection Handbook*. Three Rivers Press, NY 2003.

Peale, Norman Vincent. *Six Attitudes for Winners*. Tyndale House Publishers, Inc. Wheaton, Il 1989.

Peale, Norman Vincent. *The Power of Positive Thinking*. Ballantine Books, NY, NY 1956.

Pease, Allan and Barbara. *The Definitive Book of Body Language*. Bantam Dell. NY, NY 2004.

Perkins, John & Ridenhour, Al & Kovsky Matt. *Attack Proof: The Ultimate Guide to Personal Protection*. Human Kinetics, Champaign, IL 2000.

Pietsch, William. *HUMAN BE-ING: How to have a creative relationship instead of a power struggle*. Lawrence Hill & Company Publishers Inc, NY, NY 1974.

Personal Protection Consultants, Inc. OCAT® Instructor Manual. 2009.

Personal Protection Consultants, Inc. PATH® Instructor Manual. 2009.

Personal Safety Training Inc. AVADE® Instructor Manual. 2016.

Personal Safety Training Inc. SOCS® Trainers Manual. 2015.

PPCT Management Systems, Inc. *Defensive Tactics Instructor Manual*. PPCT 2005.

Purpura, Philip. *The Security Handbook: Second Edition*. Butterworth Heinemann, Boston, 2003.

Ratey, John J. *Spark: The Revolutionary New Science of Exercise and the Brain*. Little, Brown and Co., NY, NY 2008.

Rawls, Neal. *BE ALERT BE AWARE HAVE A PLAN: The complete guide to protecting yourself, your home, your family.* Globe Pequot Press, Guilford, CT.

Rodale Inc. *Men's Health Today 2007.* Rodale Inc. US 2007.

Sandford, John and Paula. *The Transformation of the Inner Man.* Bridge Publishing Inc. S. Plainfield, NJ 1982.

Strong, Sanford. *Strong on Defense: Survival Rules to Protect You and Your Family from Crime.* Pocket Books, NY, NY 1996.

Sjodin, Terri. *New Sales Speak: The 9 Biggest Sales Presentation Mistakes and How to Avoid Them.* Better Life Media. DVD and CD 2004.

Soo, Chee, *The Chinese Art of T'ai Chi Ch'uan: The Taoist way to mental and physical health.* The Aquarian Press, Wellingborough, Northamptonshire 1984.

Staley, Charles. *The Science of Martial Arts Training.* Multi Media Books, Burbank, CA 1999.

The Evidence Bible, NKJV, Bridge-Logos Publishers- © 2011 by Ray Comfort. Alachua, FL.

The Results Driven Manager. *Dealing with Difficult People.* Harvard Business School Publishing Corp, Boston MA 2005.

Theriault, Jean Yves. *Full Contact Karate.* Contemporary Books Inc. Chicago, 1983.

The World's Greatest Treasury of Health Secrets. Bottom Line Publications, Stamford, CT 2006.

Thompson, George. *Verbal Judo.* Quill William Morrow, NY 1993.

Tsunetomo, Yamamoto. *Hagakure: The Book of the Samurai.* Kodansha International, Tokyo, NY, London 1979.

Turner, James T. *Violence in the Medical Care Setting.* Aspen Systems Corporation, Rockville, MD 1984.

Tzu, Sun. *The Art of War.* Samuel Griffith Interpretation, Oxford University Press, 1993.

Ueshiba, Kisshomaru. *The Spirit of Aikido.* Kodansha International, Tokyo, NY, London, 1987.

Van Horne, Patrick and Riley, Jason. *LEFT of BANG: How the Marine Corps' Combat Hunter Program Can Save Your Life*. Black Irish Entertainment LLC, NY and Los Angeles, 2014.

US Dept. of Justice. *Workplace Violence: Issues in Response.* Critical Incident Response Group, National Center for the Analysis of Violent Crime, FBI Academy, Quantico, Virginia 2001.

Wallace, Bill. *The Ultimate Kick: The Wallace Method to Winning Karate.* Unique Publications, Burbank, CA 1987.

Webster, Noah. *Webster's Dictionary*. Modern Promotions/Publishers, NY, NY 1984.

Willis, Brian. *W.I.N. 2: Insights Into Training and Leading Warriors.* Warrior Spirit Books, Calgary, Alberta, Canada 2009.

Websites and Web links

http://www.AVADEtraining.com

http://www.personalsafetytraining.com

http://www.socstraining.com

http://www.tribalsecuritytraining.com

http://www.wpvprevention.com

http://www.aaets.org/article54.htm

http://en.wikipedia.org/wiki/Excited_delirium

http://en.wikipedia.org/wiki/Chemical_restraint

http://en.wikipedia.org/wiki/Positional_asphyxia

Training Courses For You And Your Agency

The only way to deal with conflict and avoid violence of any type is through awareness, vigilance, avoidance, defensive training and escape planning."

David Fowler, President of PSTI specializes in nationally recognized training programs which empower individuals, increase confidence and promote pro-active preventative solutions.

OSHA, Labor & Industries, Joint Commission, State WPV Laws, and the Dept. of Health all recognize that programs like PSTI's are excellent preventive measures to reduce crime, violence and aggression in the workplace.

www.PersonalSafetyTraining.com

PSTI Offers

On-Site Training (we will come to you!) No need to send staff away for training. PSTI will come to your place of business and train your staff.

Train-the-Trainer (Instructor Seminars)
The most cost effective way to implement PSTI training courses to your organization. We can come to you for instructor courses or you can send staff to one of our upcoming seminars.

Combo Classes
Combination classes are where basic training and instructor training are combined during on-site training. It is a great way to introduce PSTI training with our initial instruction and then continue on with your own instructors.

E-Learning
Are you looking for a healthcare solution to integrate a workplace violence prevention program in order to meet compliance standards for both State and Federal guidelines? AVADE® E-learning offers a great solution to give your staff an introductory, yet comprehensive training program that can be completed as needed.

About Us
Personal Safety Training Inc. is committed to providing the finest level of training and service to you and your employees. Whether you are an individual, or represent an agency, we have the Basic and Instructor Course Certifications that YOU need.

Contact Us
Personal Safety Training Inc.
P.O. Box 2957, Coeur d' Alene, ID 83816
(208) 664-5551—Fax (208) 664-5556

Multiple training options for your organization:

- **2 hr. Intro Courses**
- **1/2 Day Training Sessions**
- **One Day Classes**
- **Two Day Classes**
- **Train-the-Trainer (Instructor Classes)**

PSTI serves a variety of industries:

Healthcare	Corporate	Security	Gaming	Churches

TRAINING COURSES FOR YOU AND YOUR AGENCY

SOCS® (Security Oriented Customer Service)
SOCS® training teaches staff how to identify and provide great customer service while maintaining safety in the workplace. The core concept of the training is to be able to provide excellent service without having to think about it. Creating habits, skills, and taking action for exceptional customer service is the goal of the SOCS® training program.
www.SOCStraining.com

DTS™ (Defensive Tactics System)
The DTS™ training program covers basic defensive tactics, control techniques and defensive interventions. Course includes stance, movement, escort techniques, take-downs, defensive blocking, active defense skills, weapon retention, handcuffing, post incident response and documentation and much-much more.

AVADE® Personal Safety Training

Buy the ultimate book on HOW to keep you and your family safe. Call us for training. The training program is designed to increase your overall safety in all environments. The curriculum is based David Fowler's book, *Be Safe Not Sorry—the Art and Science of keeping YOU and your Family safe from crime and violence.*

AVADE® Workplace Violence Prevention

The Workplace Violence Prevention Training is offered as a Basic and Instructor level course for private corporations, healthcare, security companies' and any agency wanting to educate, prevent and mitigate the risk of violence to their employees.

Pepper Spray Defense™ Training

Tactical and Practical concepts of when and how to use pepper spray in a variety of environmental situations. Aerosol Pepper is a great less-than-lethal control and defense option for agencies that encounter violence and aggression.

Defense Baton™ Training Techniques

Training in the use of an expandable baton, straight stick or riot control baton. Techniques and topics in this training include: vulnerable areas of the body, stance, movement, blocks, control holds, counter strikes, draws and retention techniques.

Handcuffing Tactics™

Training in the use of plastic, chain or hinged handcuffs. Standing, kneeling and prone handcuffing techniques are covered. In this training course you will also learn DT fundamentals, proper positioning, nomenclature, risk factors and post incident response and documentation.

HDTS™ (Healthcare Defensive Tactics System) The HDTS™ training program for healthcare covers basic defensive tactics, control techniques and defensive interventions. Course includes stance, movement, escort techniques, take-downs, team intervention, defensive blocking, active defense skills, weapon retention, patient restraint techniques, post incident response and documentation and much-much more.

SIRS™ (Security Incident Reporting System)

A training program that teaches officers how to effectively and intelligently write security incident reports. Documentation of security incidents is absolutely critical to your agency's ability to track and trend, reduce liability and share vital information. If you're like most agencies—you know that proper, structured, effective and reliable reports save time, money and allow you to track incidents and reduce liability risk.

AVADE® Violence in the Workplace

Buy the book on HOW to be safe in the work-place. This is the text based on the AVADE® training system. Can't come to a class, at least get the book! The knowledge contained in these pages will teach YOU awareness, vigilance, avoidance, defensive interventions and escape strategies for your place of business.

PSTI Training Products

Instructor Manuals   **Student Manuals**   **Training Weapons**

PSTI Social Media

Check out our videos   **Write a review**

Contact us today for training for YOU or your Agency!

Personal Safety Training Inc.
(208) 664-5551 ~
www.PersonalSafetyTraining.com

Check out PSTI on Social Media

LinkedIn   **Google**   **Facebook**

YouTube   **Twitter**

Feedback Form
Healthcare Defensive Tactics System™ (HDTS™) Training Program

Please assist us in our continuing effort to evolve the Healthcare Defensive Tactics System™ training program to meet the unique needs of the protective services industry and the officers that serve.

?   What was the most valuable thing you learned from this training?

_____

_____

?   What other topics would you like to see?

_____

_____

?   Would you recommend this training to others?   YES   NO   NOT SURE

?   How beneficial was the HDTS™ training?   VERY   IT WAS OK   GOOD   NOT SURE

Please rate the presentation and delivery of your trainer:

Name of trainer   Low   High

_____   1   2   3   4   5   6   7   8   9   10

_____   1   2   3   4   5   6   7   8   9   10

Please rate content of the HDTS™ course: 1   2   3   4   5   6   7   8   9   10

?   Were the facilities (training area) acceptable?   YES   NO   NOT SURE

?   What HDTS™ topic/technique did you like the most?

_____

_____

?   What HDTS™ topic/technique did you like the least?

_____

_____

?.   I recommend the following changes to the HDTS™ program:

_____

_____

?   May we use your comments for marketing and testimonial purposes?   YES   NO

If yes, can we get your name: _____